SET YOUR
HOUSE IN ORDER

SET YOUR HOUSE IN ORDER

*A Practical Way
to Prepare for Death*

Miles O'Brien Riley

DOUBLEDAY & COMPANY, INC.
GARDEN CITY, NEW YORK
1980

Library of Congress Cataloging in Publication Data

Riley, Miles O'Brien, 1937–
Set your house in order.

1. Death—Miscellanea.   I. Title.
BT825.R5   248'.4
ISBN: 0-385-14326-5
Library of Congress Catalog Card Number 78–20095

My Dedication

Dear Mom and Dad,

This little book is intended for you, not to read, but to write, to help you organize some of the details of your lives. It will hopefully help you prepare for the fuller life to come.

Because you are of different faiths and have different convictions about such things as funerals, burials, and bequeathals, I will try to make it as broad and basic a workbook for death preparation as possible.

It is also for me, my six brothers and sisters, their families, and for the countless other individuals who dislike thinking or talking about death, much less preparing for it.

Fifteen years of professional experience as a priest have involved me in hundreds of negative, guilt-ridden, painful, and ill-prepared deaths—deaths that hurt and separated families when they could have healed and unified them. I want something more for you, for us.

Death is not a good thing. Christians do not look forward to death, as some sentimental preachers and counselors suggest. Death, the result of sin, is tragic and frightening. Only our belief in Christ and our faith in the Resurrection enable us to face death and accept it, sometimes painfully, almost always reluctantly.

Death is a part of life, a mystery that inspires both fear

and faith. Only those who secretly say, "I wouldn't be caught dead planning for death" are caught dead.

Your house was always a real home. Hopefully, helping you put it in order will accomplish what I have never been able to express well enough: "Thanks. I love you."

Your Son,
Miles

CONTENTS

Chapter 4 YOUR WILL

Chapter 5 YOUR WISHES

Chapter 6 YOUR FUNERAL PLANS

Chapter 7 YOUR FUNERAL SERVICE

Chapter 11 EDUCATIONAL

Chapter 1

YOU

Your Dedication

I was driving home the other night down Dolores Street, the street of sorrows, thinking how life is just that for so many people—a street of sorrows—when a bit of graffiti scrawled on the curb suddenly caught my eye. There, on the cement street divider, someone had painted in big black letters the words "I Love You."

It reminded me of a rock I found on the beach one day. Someone had written "Please Turn Me Over" in fingernail polish on the flat surface. When I did, on the reverse it said, "Thank You."

We go through life sending little messages to one another: in paint, ink, fingernail polish, and on typewriters; with flowers and homemade gifts; through our words and our deeds; with our children and our dreams.

Everything we say or do is a form of communication with someone, either in the present or in the future. How wonderful it is for both of us when our actions express "hello there," "thank you," or "I love you."

That's what God said to us with His gift of life and the gift of His Son. And that's what this little book is meant to be: a *gift*. Please pick it up and complete the following lines lovingly.

Begin here:

This book has been given to ———— by ———— because:

———— I love you and/or

———— living and dying are precious experiences and/or

———— I know you are (or are not) afraid to die and/or

2

———— you are almost as bad as I am about planning ahead and/or

———— Other: ——————————————————————

If your answer to the first fill-in line was "to me by me," you already realize that filling out this little booklet is really a gift from you to those who will have to care for matters when you die.

Twins

The twins held on to each other for dear life. They knew they were alive: aware of space, self, and each other—even the life-cord connecting them to their mother. Imagine someone loving them enough to share everything she had! They were alive, in love, and at peace. Then the changes started. Arms and legs branched out. Fingers and toes budded. They became frightened.

"What's happening, what does this mean?"

"It means we are drawing near to birth."

"But I don't want to be born. That means leaving this world behind."

"I'd like to stay here forever."

"Me, too."

"I wonder if there's life after birth."

"We'll never know. No one has ever returned."

"But if it all ends at birth, then this life is absurd."

"That's right. In fact, if that's true, then there is no mother."

"But these things were always here. Besides, have we ever seen her, ever heard her voice?"

"You mean we just invented a mother to help us feel secure and loved?"

Finally, when the mother's love could wait no longer, the twins were born to live, to die, and to live forever.

Your Practice Page

Like diets, discipline, and detachment, the hardest part of death preparation is getting started.

Try saying the word "death" out loud; then say, "I am going to die." It's easier to say than to accept. If you can say it, you can write about it. This is your book—my outline, your book. You write this one.

For practice, please fill in the names of your key advisers below. Include addresses and phone numbers if possible. Write in pencil so you can change your mind and your notes. Otherwise you'll have to go out and buy another one of these books; before long, we'll have a runaway bestseller.

Your doctor: _____

Your lawyer: _____

Your pastor or parish: _____

Your executor: _____

Your funeral director or mortuary: _____

Your banker or bank: _____

Your insurance agent or company: _____

Your closest relative: _____

Your closest friend: _____

Don't worry if you can't fill in a name and address or phone number for every blank space. I'll help you organize these matters as we go along. You never have to answer everything. Just fill out what you need—what helps you set your house in order.

Accepting My Own Death

Compassionate Friends is a national organization offering friendship and understanding to bereaved parents. The mailing address of their U.S. headquarters is P. O. Box 1347, Oakbrook, Ill. 60521. Our local chapter shared the following beautiful letter with me:

"When I was told I had leukemia it really hit hard. I had a friend who three years before died of exactly what I was now being told I had. I wanted to know how long I was going to live. I was told I would live until I was ready to die. My doctor explained that there comes a time when the good times you have aren't worth the bad. That's when you're ready to die. I didn't understand this. I watched so many of my hospital friends die. I didn't think they were ready. Then there was Joyce. Joyce had been getting morphine for bone pain for weeks. The night I saw her she was in pain. I talked to her for a while and then said good-bye. The next morning Joyce died. She was ready to die. Now I understood.

"I had become very close to the chaplain at the hospital. I'm not religious but I believe in God. The chaplain understood this. He helped me gain the courage to plan my own funeral. He said that my funeral should be the way I want it to be. Planning my funeral was difficult, but we finally got everything straight. I didn't die then. But now we have one less thing to worry about. My funeral is planned; now we can forget about it.

"Yes, death is difficult for all parties. But in the end I think it's most difficult on those who just hear the news.

Outline for Your Autobiography

When filling out this workbook planner, don't forget to write small, legibly, and in pencil so you can change and update facts.

Full name: _____

Complete address: _____

Phone(s): _____

Resident at this location since: _____ Previous address: ___

Sex: _____ Birthplace and date: _____

Citizenship: _____ Soc. Sec. No.: _____

Father's full name and birthplace: _____

Mother's maiden name and birthplace: _____

Your present marital status and past history: _____
_____

Full name and occupation of spouse: _____

Military status: dates of service, rank, branch, and service no.: _____

Your present or last occupation: _____

Type of work: _____ Employer: _____ Date: _____

Religious preference: _____ Church or synagogue: _____

Education and degrees earned: _____
_____

Accomplishments (e.g., athletic, cultural, artistic): _____
_____

Accepting My Own Death (cont'd)

Those who witness a death that's been coming can say, 'They were ready; it was time.'

"If you know someone or are someone who has trouble thinking, accepting, and talking about death, please write. I've learned to accept death and I'd like to help others do the same."

This mature, spiritual letter was written by Lori Stavcin in early April 1978, a few weeks before her death at age thirteen.

Outline for Your Autobiography (cont'd)

Honors (e.g., awards, special recognition): _____

_____

Memberships (e.g., fraternal or community organizations):

_____

Other significant information (e.g., family roots): _____

_____

Answering Service

"Hello there! . . . Thank you for calling . . . This is Father Miles's answering service . . . I'm sorry, but Father Miles is unable to come to the phone at this time . . . Please be good enough to wait for my beep tone, leave your name and number, and I will see to it that he gets your message and returns your call, if he likes you and wants to talk to you. Incidentally, you will have approximately thirty seconds to leave a message—this should be a real challenge and good preparation for a future career in radio broadcasting.

"Listen, while I have you on the line, let me be candid. I'm really sick and tired of being an answering service. It makes me feel so mechanical, so computerized, so impersonal. I mean, I know *you're* real and human, but I'm just afraid that someday you'll get an answering service like me and it'll just be us answering services talking to one another all day long. And when human communication stops, so does love.

"Well, I'd better let you go. Incidentally, if you were calling for the mass schedule, the Christmas midnight mass this year will be at midnight . . . *B-e-e-p.*"

10

A Brief Medical History

Don't let this page scare you. Provide only the information that will help others help you—to take care of things after you're gone. The entire workbook—and this section in particular—should be reviewed and updated every five (5) years. So start by filling in today's

Date: ＿＿

Name of physicians: ＿＿＿＿＿＿＿ Phone: ＿＿＿＿＿

    Generalist: ＿＿＿＿＿＿＿＿＿ Phone: ＿＿＿＿＿

    Specialist: ＿＿＿＿＿＿＿＿＿ Phone: ＿＿＿＿＿

Height: ＿＿   Weight: ＿＿   Age: ＿＿

Present state of health: ＿＿＿＿＿＿＿＿＿＿＿＿＿＿

Major illnesses: ＿＿＿＿＿＿＿＿＿＿＿＿＿＿＿＿

    Accidents: ＿＿＿＿＿＿＿＿＿＿＿＿＿＿＿＿

    Operations: ＿＿＿＿＿＿＿＿＿＿＿＿＿＿＿

    Allergies: ＿＿＿＿＿＿＿＿＿＿＿＿＿＿＿＿

Current prescribed medications: ＿＿＿＿＿＿＿＿＿

＿＿＿＿＿＿＿＿＿＿＿＿＿＿＿＿＿＿＿＿＿＿＿＿

Last complete physical examination: ＿＿＿＿＿＿＿

Donated blood, plasma (place, date): ＿＿＿＿＿＿＿

Blood type: ＿＿＿＿＿＿＿＿＿＿＿＿＿＿＿＿＿＿

For information on donating your body, internal organs, skin tissue, and so forth, see chapter entitled "Giving Yourself Away" (or, how a little extra love enables you to "live on" and help another human being).

11

Chapter 2

OTHERS

Letter from a Lover

This love letter arrived late.

I don't know why I'm writing to you. I keep telling myself it's because I want to help the next guy. Maybe I can save him from making the same mistakes I made. But deep down I know it's got to be guilt.

For twenty-three years I was married to a wonderful woman. She was twenty years my junior and I was sure she would outlive me. But I was mistaken and now she is gone. Throughout our marriage she complained because I never could say "I love you."

I kept telling her that she didn't need to hear it, that I treated her well and gave her everything she wanted, and that this should be proof enough of my love for her. But my answer never seemed to satisfy her.

She asked me at least 100 times to try to put it into words. "A woman needs to hear it," she kept saying, but I was stubborn—or insensitive—and couldn't bring myself to express my feelings for her.

If I knew then what I know now, I would say "I love you" a dozen times a day. Why don't people appreciate what they have while they still have it? Why must life's lessons always be learned through suffering—or death?

I love you.

Your Family and Special Friends

YOUR SPOUSE

Full name ——————————————— Date of Birth ———

Health ——————————————— Place of birth (state) ———

Date of marriage ——— Place of marriage ————

YOUR CHILDREN

Full Name	Son/ Daughter	Date of Birth	Health	Marital Status	No. and Age of Grand-children
———	———	———	———	———	———
———	———	———	———	———	———
———	———	———	———	———	———
———	———	———	———	———	———
———	———	———	———	———	———
———	———	———	———	———	———

OTHER DEPENDENTS

Full Name	Relationship	Date of Birth	Health	Extent of Dependency
———	———	———	———	———
———	———	———	———	———
———	———	———	———	———

Prior Marriages and Obligations ————————————

CLOSE RELATIVES AND FRIENDS

Full Name	Address	Phone Number
———	———	———
———	———	———
———	———	———
———	———	———

15

Healing Miracles

I believe in miracles not because I believe in God—I believed in God long before I believed in miracles—but because I've experienced them.

The Gospel tells us that Jesus was involved in three kinds of miracles: raisings from the dead (the widow's son, Jairus' daughter, Lazarus, and Christ's own resurrection), natural wonders, and healings.

These miracles were not magic proofs of Jesus' divinity; rather, they were signs of the Father's loving concern, inviting a response of faith.

You can see this in the many healing miracles the Father worked through Jesus—especially his death and resurrection—and still works today when the Holy Spirit overcomes the evil spirit.

We need the miracle of healing not just when we are sick, sinful, or suffering but also when we feel lonely, afraid, alienated, or dependent.

Healing is relationship: being centered and connected. The Church, like Christ, becomes a healing focus, a community inviting all of us to become healers and miracle workers.

If you believe in God, no explanation of miracles is necessary. If you don't believe in God, no explanation of miracles is possible.

People to Provide Help at Time of Death

You have already figured out that this book is not only helping you gather information and prepare for death; ultimately it is a gift from you to those who will care for all the details and arrangements when you die.

For that reason, this chapter is especially detailed and thorough so that you can help your survivors to better organize themselves! You are giving them valuable guidelines. Don't worry about every single item. The same person may handle several needs. People will improvise and be eager to help:

· To coordinate funeral services and burial (incl. church, mortuary, cemetery, and obituary notice for newspaper). This should be someone with whom you have discussed the general spirit as well as the details: _____

_____ (for details, see pp. 85–87)

· To notify family and friends (incl. lawyer and executor, as well as distant relatives or friends who will receive letter or printed notice): _____

_____ (for details, see pp. 127–29)

· To answer phone and door (keeping careful records for follow-up "thank you" notes): _____

_____

· To arrange for appropriate child or animal care: _____

_____

· To coordinate supply of food and drink (incl. shopping, cooking, and gifts of food for the next several days):

_____

_____

Mourning

Perhaps the most painful fact of life is death, either your own or that of someone you love. Certainly, the hardest fact of death is mourning.

Psychologists describe mourning as "a gradual working through of an affect or feeling which, if released in its full strength, would overwhelm the ego."

The key word is "work." Mourning is tough work. It means coming to grips with all kinds of uneasy emotions: a sense of guilt growing out of the resentment you feel because someone has died and left you alone; or because you somehow feel partially responsible for the death. (One woman used to tell her husband, "If you die and leave me with all these kids to take care of, I'll kill you!")

Other awkward emotions include relief (as when someone dies who has been ill for a long time), helplessness, anxiety, or an empty, gnawing, numb feeling.

Still, the act of mourning is good, clean, hard work, both necessary and valuable.

It's part of saying "good-bye," which literally means "God be with you."

• To arrange hospitable welcome for visiting relatives and friends: _____
_____ (for details, see pp. 127–29)

• To oversee household needs (e.g., cleaning, plants, and flower care): _____

• To serve as pallbearers (choose six individuals and make your friends with heart or back problems honorary pallbearers): _____

• To coordinate "thank you" notes for phone calls, visits, gifts, and other acts of kindness (whether handwritten or printed, these notes are hard and time-consuming to write):

• To check all life and casualty insurance, contracts, death benefits, assets and debts, wills and deeds to properties, and all key documents listed in this book to make certain someone follows up on everything promptly: ____
_____ (for details, see pp. 123–25)

(A "P.S." for those of you who will offer help and comfort at the time of death: Remember the family three months later, too, when they may need you even more!)

When You Lose a Loved One

It's hard to die. But it's harder, I think, when someone you love dies. Death isn't the only way we lose a loved one, a relative, a friend. But it is the most final.

You feel numb, hollow, hurt, hopeless, restless, listless, irritable, and sometimes even a little guilty. Shock triggers denial, which hardens into anger, which melts into depression, which blossoms into understanding and acceptance. The soul has its own natural healing process.

Make a deal with yourself not to press and push, not to try too hard. Declare a psychological cease-fire, a long emotional wind-down holiday. Decide not to decide. Stay just busy enough to avoid the bottomless pit of self-pity.

Believers feel that there is a reason for everything that happens. The kids call it karma. We used to call it God's loving providence.

We have a motto inscribed over the entrance to our communications center: "God sees you—but He understands." One of our liberated members put an "S" in front of the "H" in "He."

Your prayer might go like this: "God, I'm too down to drag myself to church today. Please make a house call."

People to Be Notified When You Die

NAMES   ADDRESSES

Doctor: _____

Pastor: _____

Executor: _____

Lawyer: _____

Financial advisor: _____

Funeral director: _____

Cemetery director: _____

Living transplant bank: _____

Employer: _____

Landlord (to notify utilities companies and post office if you live alone): _____

Distant relatives and friends (phone to find out if they might attend the funeral; otherwise send a note or printed announcement): _____

_____

_____

At the time of your death the attending doctor or county coroner will make out a death certificate. The funeral director you indicate will then remove the body. He should already have a copy of your instructions, indicating what type of services are wanted. If he does not, or if a different mortician is called, you should keep a copy of such arrangements at home in this book, where family or friends can easily find it—because you will have told them that this is one of your last gifts to them!

Your priest, minister, or rabbi should then be notified. In most cases, your religious readiness for death—both spiritual preparation and funeral arrangements—has been attended to. If not, then this week is the perfect time to call and make a date for a warm, honest, friendly talk with your favorite religious adviser. Now where is that phone number?

Chapter 3

YOUR THINGS

If You Were to Die

If you were to die today, what would you want written on your tombstone? How would you compose your own epitaph?

If you were to die today, how would you want your obituary to read? What will that single short paragraph in the local newspaper say about your life, your accomplishments, your values, and your goals? What have you left behind in this world?

If you can imagine yourself lying there in your coffin, who would come to visit and offer a prayer? What would they say? What would they be thinking?

If you were to die today, would there be any loose ends in your life? Any unfinished business? Anything you never quite got around to doing? Any forgotten thank-yous or good-byes?

If you were to die today, would you be ready to meet God? What is the first question you would want to ask? Would you have any complaints, suggestions, special gratitude? Who would you be most anxious to see?

If you were to die today, who would miss you most? Whom would you miss most?

If your answer to all of the above is "I don't know," that will remind you: We don't know "the day or the hour" either.

Documenting Your Property

This is your big test; if you can handle this section, the rest of this workbook will be easy. The following valuable documents will be needed for insurance, pensions, social security, as well as legal proof of age, ownership, place of birth, religious affiliation, relationships, and so forth. Please give complete locations and write clearly. If you are not a terribly organized person, think of this section as a treasure hunt (or, better, an Easter egg hunt, since you are preparing for resurrection and eternity). Here is your map:

DOCUMENT	LOCATION
Will	_____
Safe deposit box	_____
Key for safe deposit box	_____
Birth certificate	_____
Baptism (confirmation) certificate	_____
Bankbook(s)	_____
Checkbook(s)	_____
Insurance policies	_____
Stocks, bonds, U. S. Government bonds	_____
Mortgages, notes, agreements, contracts	_____
Deed(s) to property; bill of sale	_____
Income tax returns; tax receipts	_____
Patents, copyrights	_____
Veteran's discharge certificate	_____
Marriage certificate	_____

There, now, isn't that a great feeling of accomplishment and completion! Incidentally, how many of the above can you store in one drawer or file? Please put as many as possible in one place.

Kingdom Come

"Thy Kingdom Come" we pray in the Our Father, meaning the Kingdom of Heaven, the Kingdom of God.

We know that the Kingdom had already begun, or dawned with, Jesus, and will come full circle only in our own resurrection, when we are in Heaven, in God.

You will know that the Kingdom of God is here when the deaf hear, the blind see, and the lame walk. And Jesus says to tell John the Baptizer that it's already happening right here, right now!

But the radical part, at least in Jesus' day, was that he was promising the Kingdom to the poor. Jewish leaders, the hierarchy, and the religious ethic of the time all said to the poor and the powerless, the sick and the sinful "You're damned."

And Jesus came along and said the opposite: "You're saved" (not tomorrow, but now); "You're forgiven (*before*, not after; *given*, not repaid)."

And who does he say it to? The people at the bus depot. The people on the streetcar. The people at the supermarket, the clinic, the bar, and at St. Anthony's Dining Room, with their St. Vincent de Paul wardrobes.

To the poor, ordinary folks he says, "The Kingdom of God is yours." While the rest of us pray: "Thy Kingdom Come."

Your Property

It will be most helpful to collect in one place information regarding all your property. You have more than you realize! If any section does not apply, skip it. If you need additional space, write in the margins or attach index cards with the appropriate information. Remember, if you are having trouble organizing this financial information, imagine what your family and friends would have to go through without this handy outline!

SCHEDULE A CASH AND BANK ACCOUNTS

Type	Self	Spouse	Joint	Total
1.				
2.				
3.				
4.				
5.				
6.				
7.				
8.				

Take It with You

A dying father called his three grown sons to his bedside. "Boys," he said, "you are successful now—doctor, lawyer, and sales manager. I have one simple request: When I die —and of course all my wealth will be yours—I ask each of you, as a sign of filial devotion and gratitude, to put a thousand dollars into my coffin." They all agreed, somewhat bewildered.

A short time thereafter the father died. His sons went to the mortuary. The eldest son, the doctor, went up to the body, said a prayer, and put a thousand dollars in one-hundred-dollar bills into the folds of the coffin. The lawyer came up next. He had a thousand dollars in smaller bills; he rolled these up neatly and put them in the coffin. A bit later the youngest son, the sales manager, approached, said a short prayer, wrote a check for three thousand dollars, tucked it in the coffin, and took the two thousand dollars in cash.

The moral of the story is: You can't take it with you, but you can send ahead—and open an account—through prayer.

Your Property (cont'd)

SCHEDULE B   STOCKS

Name and Number	*Units and Value*	*Broker*
1.		
2.		
3.		
4.		
5.		
6.		

SCHEDULE C   BONDS

Name and Number	*Units and Value*	*Broker*
1.		
2.		
3.		
4.		
5.		
6.		

What Do You Want?

What do you want?

Okay, now what do you really want?

Yes, that too! But, at the deepest level, way down deep inside . . .

What do you want?

I mean when you're together, when you're at your very best, what do you really want?

To be free—free from fear, from self-conscious human respect, from insensitivity—free to dream, trust, grow, risk?

To be vulnerable—to love, to be loved, to be gentle, to be weak, to need, to cry, to feel . . .

To be creative—to be funny, imaginative, outrageous, refreshing, playful, wonder-filled?

To matter, to contribute, to be needed, to be concerned, involved?

To be whole, holy, healthy, happy?

To live forever?

If any or all of the above is what you really and truly want, then I have a suggestion for you.

And his first name is Jesus.

And what he really wants is you!

Your Property (cont'd)

SCHEDULE D PERSONAL NOTES, ACCOUNTS RECEIVABLE, MORTGAGES

Type	Present Value	How Payable
1.		
2.		
3.		
4.		
5.		
6.		

By now you may be so frustrated that you are about to pray that age-old infallible prayer to Almighty God: "Help!"

Don't be too proud or too parsimonious to seek additional help from an accountant or attorney if your financial affairs are more than you can handle.

Tags

Right now I'm looking at a wonderful old bookcase that belonged to my grandfather. Fashioned of rich, dark mahogany wood, it has four sections or shelves, each covered by a magnificent leaded glass window mounted on hinges. It stands five feet tall and stood out even amidst the antique grandeur of grandfather's study.

Our lives and homes are filled with objects of art—some practical, some silly, some simply marvelous memories. How many of these things, passing from generation to generation, tell a special story! It's a shame when those stories get lost or forgotten in the shuffle!

One way to record these precious memories is to glue a tag under or on the back of pieces of furniture, statues, paintings, and memorabilia. This might be a small slip of paper relating the origin or value of an object, or a note stating, "Uncle Charlie McCloud brought this home from China" or "We picked this up for a song in New Mexico—but don't let it go for a song. I was offered three hundred dollars for it in '68. . . ."

Sometimes sentimental history is the real family treasure. A little tag can jog the memory.

Your Property (cont'd)

In describing your "real" property below, you may also want to include the following: name in which title is held, purchase date, original investment, any mortgages or leases, and so forth. Or you may just prefer to fill in the basics.

SCHEDULE E   REAL ESTATE

	Description	*Location*	*Mortgage*	*Market Value*
1.				
2.				
3.				
4.				

SCHEDULE F   PERSONAL PROPERTY

(e.g., cars, TV, stereo, furniture, jewelry, coins, art or other collections)

	Description	*Location*	*Payment Due*	*True Value*
1.				
2.				
3.				
4.				

PERSONAL MEMENTOS

I wish to leave the following mementos (e.g., family album, sewing box, and family Bible to my nephew Tim) to those indicated below:

1. _____ to _____
2. _____ to _____
3. _____ to _____

What's It All About?

Jimi Hendrix, one of the most famous rock-and-roll musicians of our age, suddenly interrupted one of his giant live concerts to ask the audience, "Anyone know what life is all about?" No one moved. No one answered.

Perhaps people thought it was a joke, a hype, or a part of the act. Perhaps no one was ready to give a serious answer to a serious question at that moment.

What if you had been there . . . and Jimi Hendrix suddenly stopped and asked you, "Hey, do you know what life is all about?" What would you have said? How would you have answered?

To know, love, and serve God? To be happy here and forever? To find peace? To help others? To save your soul? What would your response have been?

It might be a good idea to have an answer ready. I wish someone had had an answer for Jimi. Three weeks later he died from an overdose of drugs—and that's not the answer!

Your Property (cont'd)

SCHEDULE G   INSURANCE

(e.g., life,* health, fire, auto, etc.)

Even if this workbook is starting to feel like an income tax return, don't despair. You only have to fill out this book and your life once!

	Company	Kind	Insured	Amount
1.				
2.				
3.				
4.				
5.				
6.				
7.				
8.				
9.				
10.				

* Life insurance has an important place in any estate since it provides two important kinds of estate protection. First, it provides immediate, tax-exempt funds for burial expenses, doctor's bills, court costs, the clearing up of personal debts, mortgage, rent, estate taxes, and other expenses that must be met at once. In this connection, insurance firms take pride in the promptness with which they pay the beneficiaries of life insurance. A phone call to the company office or agent is usually sufficient to initiate action on your claim. The second, long range intention of life insurance is to provide lifetime support for survivors, to guarantee a college education for your children, to set up a trust fund, to provide income for relatives, for purposes of charity, and so forth.

Retirement

Frankly, we just aren't ready for it.

You know the scene. It's Dad's first week home after retirement. Forty-three years of somehow getting out of bed, gulping down a cup of coffee or a bromo, and rushing to work. Now, for the first time, he's slouching around the house aimlessly, unshaven, rereading the sports pages, and viewing the various vicarious victims on daytime TV. Nobody knows what to do with him—including himself.

One mom handled it beautifully. After several days of this nonsense, she finally turned to her beloved and said, "Listen, honey, when I married you I vowed 'for better or for worse'—but not for lunch!"

The point is that none of us is ready for retirement. We spend our whole lives in the relatively comfortable pattern of working, raising a family, and following a set schedule. We are ready to handle any emergency except retirement. We forget to develop interests, skills, hobbies, and plans to cope with the sudden rush of freedom.

So plan ahead. In fact, it's a good idea to plan forever.

Your Property (cont'd)

SCHEDULE H   BUSINESS INTERESTS

This section might include: interest in a co-partnership; interest in life insurance on the life of another; interest in an unincorporated business; debts owed to you by others; amounts due you from claims, rights, royalties, leaseholds, judgments, remainder interest, shares in trust funds, farm products, profits resulting from growing crops or raising livestock, or farm machinery; or simpler interests like owning a fast-food franchise or a hotel on Park Place.

	Name	*Type*	*Percentage of Ownership*
1.			
2.			
3.			
4.			
5.			
6.			
7.			
8.			
9.			
10.			

Why Worry?

Yesterday I met Sam, a delightful, bubbly, energetic seventy-five-year-old believer with a sense of humor. He was in church, praying with a suspicious smile on his face, when I happened to walk down the center aisle. Sam jumped up and leaned across two lovely ladies (somewhat taken aback) to grab my hand and introduce himself.

Smiling Sam is one of those rare, glorious people who mellow with age like good wine rather than atrophy and harden like brittle charcoal. He's impish, relaxed, at peace, hope-filled—even during moments of discouragement. (With his dear wife in a convalescent hospital, he has his down days!)

Sam has a plaque on his bedroom wall that sums up his simple philosophy:

> Why Worry?
> There are only two things to worry about.
> You are either sick or you are well.
> If you are well, then there's nothing to worry
> about.
> If you are sick, you will either get well or you will
> die.
> If you get well, there's nothing to worry about.
> If you die, there are only two things to worry
> about.
> You will either go to Heaven or Hell.
> If you go to Heaven, there's nothing to worry
> about.
> But if you go to Hell, you will be so damned busy
> shaking hands with friends, you won't have
> time to worry.

38

Your Property (cont'd)

SCHEDULE I   LIABILITIES

The ideal situation is to clear up all your debts before you die. But most of us will leave this world owing something to someone. So this is a good place to make a complete list (using pencil, of course) of what you owe and to whom.

Be sure to include today's date: _____ (This way you can update your records every five years or whenever you pay your debts.) Include any of the following that apply: real-estate mortgages, estate contracts, notes payable, bank loans, credit-union loans, finance-company loans, personal loans from friends or relatives, time-payment accounts, lawsuits, claims, and so forth.

	Description	*Payee*	*How Payable*
1.			
2.			
3.			
4.			
5.			
6.			
7.			
8.			
9.			
10.			

Lost: One Wife

The following ad appeared in the lost-and-found column of a P.T.A. newspaper:

> Lost, one wife. Last seen headed to or from: school-board meeting, or garden-club meeting, or knitting club meeting, or parents' club meeting, or parish conference, or Boy Scout rally, or P.T.A. envelope stuffing, or sisterhood smorgasbord, or city council protest, or peace pray-in, or save-the-library sit-in, or save-the-bridge walkover, or save-the-bay swim-in, or clean-the-streets bend-over, or pave-the-pavement parade . . .
> Please come home!
> Am afraid to stay in the house all by myself,
>
> > Your loving husband
>
> P.S. Our marriage license may have expired.

Of course, the same kind of advertisement could be placed in the lost-and-found column by many wives in search of their husbands.

Your Property (cont'd)

SCHEDULE J CREDIT CARDS, CHARGE ACCOUNTS,
AND SUBSCRIPTIONS

Someone has already been chosen (p. 19) to help tidy up your minor financial affairs. All stores, gas companies, and credit-card companies should be notified of your death. If all your accounts are paid up, the cards should be folded, stapled, and mutilated (great fun). List your cards here:

	Company	Card Number	Limitation	*Address and Phone Number*
1.				
2.				
3.				
4.				
5.				
6.				

Also, please cancel the following subscriptions (newspapers, magazines, book and record clubs):

1. _____
2. _____
3. _____
4. _____
5. _____
6. _____

Junk

There is a great word for things of no value. We call them junk. Junk is stuff that does not matter. Junk is stuff that has been thrown away. Junk is useless, broken, and sometimes bad. Some people throw junk in a garbage heap. Some people store junk in the attic or garage. Some people shoot junk in their veins. Some people—the saddest people —think they *are* junk.

Isn't it ironic that we allow our kids to eat junk, watch junk, listen to junk, talk junk, play with junk—and then are surprised when they become "junkies"?

Maybe there's room in our world for junk. But there's no room for junk in people.

Because *God* made people.

And God doesn't make junk.

Your Physical Home

Here are a few practical odd items for your attention—to show extra thoughtfulness.

If you have ever been responsible for disposing of the effects of someone you love who has recently died, you know how painful a task this is. It is also one of the least necessary tasks. For, if we are really ready to set about preparing ourselves for the death that we say is inevitable, we owe it to our survivors to take serious stock of what kind of mess we are leaving them to plow through, clean up, parcel out and—even in the most loving families—squabble over and feel bitter about.

Closets, chests, drawers, file cabinets, garment bags, boxes, trunks, bookshelves, envelopes, piles, and stacks in attics, basements, storerooms, backrooms, garages, and sheds. Even the poorest among us accumulate possessions that we never look at, touch, use, read, refer to, or even remember. We all say with certainty that we are "going to get to that one day," but in reality we never do. We die and someone else confronts our clutter—ultimately considers it "junk," and throws most of it out.

If you can face this prospect realistically and physically begin to set your house in order right now, you are leaving your loved ones an extra gift and giving yourself some extra space.

Chapter 4

YOUR WILL

Be Right with You, Lord

When Jesus called the first potential Christians to follow him, one young man responded, "as soon as my father dies." Another said, "I'll follow you Lord, but first I have to say good-bye to my family."

We have the same problem today. We want to follow the Lord to peace and happiness, to give of ourselves with total dedication, but we always have a few more things we must do first. Thus, we, too, keep answering, "Be right with you, Lord!"

. . . as soon as my mom dies.

. . . as soon as my kids get through school.

. . . as soon as I get a better job and a little more financial security for my family.

. . . as soon as I take that vacation trip and do all those things I've always wanted to do.

. . . as soon as I resolve my grudges against a couple of people I can't stand.

. . . as soon as I get over my self-consciousness and fear of being robbed, mugged, or taken advantage of.

. . . as soon as I correct a few bad habits.

. . . as soon as I find a priest or sister I like.

. . . as soon as I find a church that makes me feel good or a confessor I can trust and talk to.

. . . as soon as I understand God's Word a little better.

. . . as soon as I become a little holier.

. . . as soon as I get everything organized.

"Be right with you, Lord!" In answering this way, we are secretly hoping, of course, that when we finally get there, He doesn't say, "Be right with you."

Where There's a Will

Most Americans have not written wills because they think wills are for older people, rich people, or people with disagreeable relatives. Wrong! Every adult who owns anything at all and cares what happens to his/her property at the time of death needs a will. Don't put if off any longer. Don't get caught dead. Then it's too late.

The following is not meant to be a substitute, or even an outline, for your will, just a few reminders:

· See a lawyer. It's worth the fifty- or hundred-dollar fee for drawing up a simple will. The preprinted form or handwritten or oral wills are just too risky in this age of legal meticulousness and minutiae. If you don't have a will, the state will distribute your properties, perhaps without adequate regard for what you might have preferred.

· Make sure someone close to you knows where to get a copy of your will shortly after your death. Since all pertinent information and instructions are outlined in these pages, you will cover everything by telling two or three trusted family friends where to find this little book.

· Review your will and legal arrangements every few years to keep up with changing laws and thus avoid complications. Also, if you move to another state, be sure to have an attorney in that state review your will.

(continued)

Heaven's Doors

A delightful little apocryphal story relates how a man arrived at Heaven's gates to discover a whole series of huge doors.

He pulled St. Peter aside and asked, "Pete, I didn't realize Heaven was like this. What are all these doors? Where do they lead?"

Peter explained: "These doors lead to the various rooms in Heaven. Each person passes through a special door."

"Who's behind that door?" the man asked.

"That's the room for Moslems and believers in Islam."

"Wow, I didn't know they were here. And who's behind that door?"

"That's for Hindus and Buddhists."

"They're here, too? And whose door is that?"

"That's the door for Jews."

"And who's over there?"

"That's the door for Protestants: Lutherans, Methodists, Presbyterians."

"And who's behind that door over there?"

"Shh . . . That's the door for Catholics. They think they're the only ones here!"

I'll bet we're all in for a surprise or two when we get to Heaven's doors.

Where There's a Will (cont'd)

· You may also be able to get your attorney to suggest exactly how best to use your assets to pay off your loans, debts, and so forth.

· Because of huge estate taxes, fees, or commissions levied on your property and bequests, you may need to explore alternatives with your legal adviser (e.g., a lawyer who specializes in estate planning can provide advice on how to minimize the impact of death taxes on your estate). This whole frightening area of taxes demands careful, long-range estate planning with your lawyer, certified public accountant, or other experts!

Other items to be specifically covered in your will:
· Executor: responsible for all final arrangements _____
_____ (cf. pp. 123–25) _____
· Guardian for children: in the event that you die before they reach legal age _____
· Persons or organizations who should be remembered: (family, friends, church, charities) _____
_____
· Principal properties to be distributed (see appropriate list in this book, pp. 25–47) _____
· Funeral instructions, bequeathals, and burial arrangements are better covered in this book than in your will since wills are not always read before burial. (Wills should *never* be kept in your safe-deposit box!)
· Note here the date of execution _____ and location _____ of your will.

Muggings

God always sends me a special grace gift on the anniversary of my ordination. This year I got mugged. Two sick thieves beat me until I begged for my life. Then they knocked me unconscious and left me bleeding in the downstairs bathroom of one of our finest hotels.

I give you these details because the first question everyone asked later was, "Where were you?"—as if place made any difference. (I had already been mugged twice in the rectory—and once in the church!)

The second question was always, "Were you wearing your collar?"—as if clerical garb was some sort of magic protection against mindless impersonal violence, which is always born of impotence.

The third question, inevitably, was even more unhelpful: "What color were your attackers?" Some people still don't realize that disease is colorless—or multicolored.

My anniversary experience taught me a great deal. I learned how precious and tenuous is God's gift of life, which we usually take for granted. I learned how vulnerable we are, no matter how careful we are, and how we need to trust in the Lord.

I learned again that the power of forgiveness—I am reminded of Jesus' last words on the cross, "Father, forgive them; they don't know what they're doing"—is so much more effective than an eye-for-an-eye form of vengeance, which you have to carry around inside you like the pus of hatred.

I learned again the overwhelming power and presence of love. Two thugs beat me unconscious, but twenty people

Ten Commandments for Wills

1. Do it! More than 70 per cent of the 1.9 million Americans who died in 1975 left no will. Wives and single people are especially remiss in this area.

2. Don't do it yourself! Holographic (i.e., handwritten) wills are legal in fewer than half of the states; even in those states, it's not always easy to establish the validity of a handwritten will. Oral wills are normally valid only if made during military combat, though some states also recognize oral wills made during a terminal illness.

3. If you want to disinherit someone, be explicit. Otherwise a disgruntled family member may be able to persuade a court that you had a lapse of memory. If this person succeeds, it could entitle him/her to a statutory interest in your estate. One imaginative woman handled it this way: "My cousin Frank always wondered if he would be mentioned in my will. Well, he is. 'Hello, Frank!' "

4. If you move to another state or buy property there, make sure your will meets that state's requirements. The requirements for a valid will may vary from state to state.

5. Review your will if your family or financial circumstances have changed since you drew it up. A marriage, divorce, death, new children or grandchildren —or a substantial change in your net worth—should prompt you to reconsider just how you want your estate to be divided.

had compassion and cared for me that night. So love won out after all!

And I learned that the few sick individuals cannot be allowed to determine our life-style, our freedom, our behavior. Evil is real, inside and all around us, but evil or sin has been conquered by Christ. There is nothing that can scare us to death.

We are free, alive, and loved.

Incidentally, fellows, I'm fine now.

Ten Commandments for Wills (cont'd)

6. Reconsider your choice of executor regularly. Choose someone who is well enough to carry out the duties of an executor (cf. pp. 123–25). It is also wise to name an alternate executor in case the first person you've designated can't or won't serve. Give your executor complete flexibility. Express your feelings and wishes candidly.
7. Specify what should happen if an heir dies before you do—or at the same time. Name a second, or even a third, beneficiary who will inherit the bequest if the first beneficiary has died.
8. Don't hide your will or leave it stashed in a safe-deposit box. In many states your safe-deposit box must be sealed at the time of your death and can't be opened for a specified period of time without a court order—a process that can be expensive and time-consuming.
9. If you make a new will, remember that a new will does not automatically supplant the old one. You may want to keep the old one, but indicate that it has been superseded by the new will.
10. Don't omit anything. Think taxes. Check out trust funds. Reward special thoughtfulness. Give confidentially, and remember those worthy causes you were interested in during your lifetime (e.g., charities, community groups, churches, schools, missions).

Bumper Stickers

Ours is an age of communication. From weekend growth groups and interpersonal sensitivity dynamics to citizen-band radios and satellites, the modern person reaches out —almost compulsively—to communicate.

One of the most intriguing and bizarre forms of mass communication is the bumper sticker—halfway between wall graffiti and Captain Marvel decals. You won't believe this, but I recently saw a station wagon whose entire back end was plastered with almost thirty of these delightful little stickers.

Herewith a random sampling: "If you love Jesus, you will prosper" . . . "If your God is dead, try mine: Jesus lives" . . . "If you love Jesus, honk twice" . . . "God isn't dead; I talked with Him this morning" . . . "Life is fragile; handle with prayer" . . . and "This is a God Squad car"— everything but an "I found it" sticker.

I had the distinct impression that the owners of that station wagon were Christians—and they were not embarrassed or hesitant to tell the whole world! Even if it is a little like wearing your faith on your sleeve (or on your bumper) and a wee bit gaudy or commercial, I'm for it.

But imagine the pressure it puts on them: They must drive like Christians, talk like Christians, act like Christians, and be like Christians . . . Christians, keep trucking!

Chapter 5

YOUR WISHES

Telegift

Maybe you are lucky enough to have an old brown-tinted photo of your great grandfather or grandmother. If only that picture could come alive and talk, tell you about your roots, your heritage, and your family tree. Your grandparents could reveal their hopes and dreams for you, their problems and concerns, memories and values. What a precious gift for family reunions and celebrations! What an education for future generations!

At least one group in the country is making this possible. The Communications Center in San Francisco helps people prepare and televise a personal memorial, a video visit with a relative or friend who is getting too old to travel or perhaps is even dying. They call it "Telegift." It consists of a twenty-to-thirty minute video cassette (¾"/color) produced and edited to create a lasting, living memory of that special person who is able to share his/her life's lessons and loves for years to come.

A hand-held portable video camera is not as frightening as a still camera or a motion picture camera and lights. The average price is several hundred dollars for the finished "Telegift" cassette. If this seems too difficult for you or yours, you might consider making an audio cassette tape recording of your own memory message. (Our night janitor just came by and asked what I was doing. When I told him about this book, he sat down and described a family he knew who taped conversations with their mom the last six months of her life. How many mothers would take the trouble to make their own recordings?) At the very least, sit down when you are in a mellow, reminiscent mood and compose a long letter to family and friends. It's a wonderful way to share the meaning of your life with those who care most about you. It's also a great opportunity to say some of the thank yous you never quite get around to this side of Heaven.

Your Spiritual Legacy

After you have tidied up all your properties, possessions, and papers, made out a legal will, and filled out all the sections concerned with your death, funeral, burial, and bequeathals, you may want to consider the extra special plus of a "spiritual legacy."

Many people will talk about you after you die—almost all of them positively, with love, gratitude, and happy memories. The most moving and meaningful talks I have heard at funerals and wakes were given not by priests or ministers (who usually do not know you that well and sometimes tend to sentimentalize) but by members of the family who found the courage to share deep feelings and personal reminiscences.

But I often wonder: If the dead person could come back for just fifteen minutes, what would he or she say? Besides telling us about God, Heaven, or the experience of dying— which so many of those who "almost died" have tried to do in recent years—what would these people say about themselves, about their lives and, especially, about and to us?

This chapter is your chance to do just that! Sit down in front of a videocamera (the "Telegift" section in this book tells you how you can make a short videotape for the many generations to come after you), a microphone (it is relatively easy to borrow someone's tape recorder or dictaphone and make a simple recording of your own voice), or at least a piece of paper—and make your own spiritual legacy.

These Horrible Forms

All these forms are beginning to get to you, right? Well, it could be worse! If you have ever experienced the panic and confusion of a traffic accident, you know how hard it is to describe what happened in a few words on one of those insurance forms or accident reports. The following are a few actual examples:

"To avoid hitting the bumper of the car in front, I struck the pedestrian."

"I told the police that I was not injured, but upon removing my hat I found that I had a skull fracture."

"The telephone pole was approaching fast. I was attempting to swerve out of its path when it struck my front end."

"Coming home, I drove into the wrong house and collided with a tree I don't have."

"An invisible car came out of nowhere, struck my vehicle, and vanished!"

"The pedestrian had no idea which way to go, so I ran over him."

"I saw the slow-moving, sad-faced old gentleman as he bounced off the hood of my car."

"The indirect cause of this accident was a little guy in a small car with a big mouth."

"I was thrown from my car as it left the road. I was later found in a ditch by some stray cows."

"The guy was all over the road. I had to swerve a number of times before I hit him."

"I pulled away from the side of the road, glanced at my mother-in-law, and headed over the embankment."

(continued)

Sample Legacy Outline

Your Spiritual Legacy might include:

· What you have learned from life: _____

_____

_____

_____

_____

· Any regrets or forgiveness to ask: _____

_____

_____

_____

· Those who touched you most deeply: _____

_____

_____

_____

· Your most precious values, experiences, memories: _____

_____

_____

_____

_____

"I had been driving my car for over forty years when I fell asleep at the wheel and had an accident."

"I was on my way to the doctor's office with rear-end trouble, when my universal joint gave way, causing me to have an accident."

Please drive (and live) carefully, for God's sake! And keep filling out these horrible forms with a smile.

· What you wanted to accomplish in life and now wish to leave to others and the world: _____

_____

_____

_____

_____

· Your highest hopes and dreams for those who come after you: _____

_____

_____

_____

_____

· The meaning of life and death for you: _____

_____

_____

_____

_____

_____

_____

NOTE: Please tuck in separate sheets of paper here, if your answers require more space. Obviously, a complete response to any of these questions would fill an entire book.

Love Stops the Clock

Why is it that everyone wants to go to Heaven—but no one wants to die?

Why is it that we all want to live forever—but we're not sure about the rest of the day?

Why do we hope for a long, full life and then live as if we wanted life to be short and shallow? We complain that "time flies," yet we constantly look for "pastimes."

We try to "stop the clock" with health and beauty aids—drugs, diets, cosmetics, and camouflage—while we overeat, undersleep, exercise wildly, and race through the day ingesting caffeine, nicotine, sugar, and alcohol.

We know that each year of our lives is passing more quickly, that we're on an up-and-down roller-coaster collision course with some final fate—and that part of us wants to get there and part wants to get off. We need some daylight "wasting" time to stop, meet, and learn to love again.

Don't just do something. Stand there. Stand up, stand under, understand that love means "wasting" time with a flower or a friend. And, of course, only love can stop the clock.

Believers know the way, the truth, and the life. They know that our final destination and the route leading there are one, that the answer to what, where, who, why and how is love.

Or Love!

And, remember, we're all in this alone . . . stop . . . and together . . . start.

Natural Death Directive

If you wish to die humanely and not be kept alive through extraordinary measures when there is no serious hope of recovery, please make an advance decision to this effect not only to assure that your wishes will be carried out but also to protect your doctors and nurses from possible legal action and to avoid leaving your survivors with a sense of guilt. Then fill out a statement similar to the one below:

TO MY FAMILY, MY PHYSICIAN, MY LAWYER, MY CLERGYMAN, TO MY MEDICAL FACILITY IN WHOSE CARE I HAPPEN TO BE, TO ANY INDIVIDUAL WHO MAY BECOME RESPONSIBLE FOR MY HEALTH, WELFARE, OR AFFAIRS:

Death is as much a reality as birth, growth, maturity, and old age—it is the certainty of life. If the time comes when I, _____, can no longer take part in decisions concerning my future, let this statement stand as an expression of my wishes while I am still of sound mind. If a situation should arise in which there is no reasonable expectation of my recovery from serious physical or mental incapacitation, I request that *I be allowed to die* and not be kept alive by artificial means or heroic measures. I do not fear death itself as much as the indignities of deterioration, dependence, and hopeless pain. I therefore ask that medication be mercifully administered to me to alleviate suffering even if this may hasten the moment of death.

Unburied Dead

In order to construct a new freeway in middle America not long ago, engineers had to move a cemetery. This required digging up what was left of the coffins and repackaging bones and ashes for relocation. What they discovered, to their horror, was the fact that a number of coffin covers had great scratch marks on the inside. Evidently some people who were pronounced dead had been buried alive, and had tried to claw their way out.

Today we have much more sophisticated ways of determining death. Still, we shudder at the thought of being buried but not yet dead.

Equally horrible is the reverse: being dead but not yet buried. Surprisingly, there are increasing examples of unburied dead. For example, people die but we don't let go, we just can't "put them to rest." Or more obvious is the case where people are kept alive like balloons at the end of an air hose. Modern medicine doesn't always know how or when to bury the dead.

But the saddest example of those who are dead but not yet buried are those unfortunate people who have lost hope.

For the grace to live and die gracefully, let us pray.

Natural Death Directive (cont'd)

This request is made after careful consideration. I hope those who care for me will feel morally bound to follow its mandate. I realize that this appears to place a heavy responsibility upon certain individuals, but it is with the intention of relieving them of such responsibility and of placing it upon myself, in accordance with my strong convictions, that this statement is made.

Signed _____

Date (should be renewed and initialed periodically) ____

Witness _____

Witness _____

Copies of this directive have been given to:

_____   _____
_____   _____
_____   _____
_____   _____

P.S. This is not euthanasia or mercy killing, which are both illegal and immoral. In any case, consult your attorney to see whether your state recognizes this type of "living will," or whether another special form is recommended. (The legal form for the state of California is reprinted on page 67.)

Harmony

The Japanese have an interesting and effective approach to happiness and self-fulfillment.

They take seven strong emotions: hate, adoration, joy, anxiety, anger, grief, and fear.

Then they work at controlling these feelings through patience and self-mastery.

This produces what the Japanese would call harmony and what we might call peace.

When the virtue of courage is added to this harmony, the Japanese believe they have achieved power.

If the Japanese want to overthrow an adversary, they simply work at upsetting his emotions, throw him off balance, get him to lose his patience, and thereby destroy his inner harmony.

Mathematically, the equation reads: hate, adoration, joy, anger, anxiety, grief, and fear + patience = harmony; harmony + courage = strength.

It's not hard to translate this into Christian Gospel. It *is* hard to translate this into Christian action.

Directive to Physicians

Directive made this _____ day of _____ (month, year).

I _____, being of sound mind, willfully, and voluntarily make known my desire that my life shall not be artificially prolonged under the circumstances set forth below, do hereby declare:

1. If at any time I should have an incurable injury, disease, or illness certified to be a terminal condition by two physicians, and where the application of life-sustaining procedures would-serve only to artificially prolong the moment of my death and where my physician determines that my death is imminent whether or not life-sustaining procedures are utilized, I direct that such procedures be withheld or withdrawn, and that I be permitted to die naturally.

2. In the absence of my ability to give directions regarding the use of such life-sustaining procedures, it is my intention that this directive shall be honored by my family and physician(s) as the final expression of my legal right to refuse medical or surgical treatment and accept the consequences from such refusal.

3. If I have been diagnosed as pregnant and that diagnosis is known to my physician, this directive shall have no force or effect during the course of my pregnancy.

4. I have been diagnosed and notified at least 14 days ago as having a terminal condition by

_____, M.D., whose address is _____

_____, and whose telephone number is _____
I understand that if I have not filled in the physician's name and address, it shall be presumed that I did not have a terminal condition when I made out this directive.

5. This directive shall have no force or effect five years from the date filled in above.

6. I understand the full import of this directive and I am emotionally and mentally competent to make this directive.

Signed _____

City, County and State of Residence _____

_____

The declarant has been personally known to me and I believe him or her to be of sound mind.

Witness _____

Witness _____

This Directive complies in form with the "Natural Death Act" California Health and Safety Code, Section 7188, Assembly Bill 3060 (Keene).

The Whole Truth

This is a very personal option and will generate as much controversy as it will peace of mind. But it's something I feel strongly about. Decide for yourself. (Perhaps this should be appended to your "living will" or "Natural Death Directive" since it seems to be the only way to let those who love and care for you know your wishes and convictions *before* the final event occurs.)

A cloak of secrecy often surrounds the fact of dying. It appears to be a well-intentioned and sometimes justified conspiracy to keep the person who is dying from full knowledge of the truth. Whether inspired by too many sentimental TV suspense stories or our own fear of death and our reluctance to face reality, maintaining secrets about terminal cancer and other illnesses is usually ill-advised. It often takes more love and courage on the part of doctors and family members to tell the whole truth.

If you feel that such knowledge would not impair your will to live and might actually help you prepare for death, you may want to indicate that fact here:

I would like to know if I am dying: yes——no——

Your next step is to let your family, friends, and doctor know how you feel. Tell them you want them to level with you. Few doctors in this country would keep the fact of a fatal illness from their patients. Ask your doctors if they ever hesitate to inform their patients.

How the fact of dying is communicated to you and how you and your physicians jointly plan to deal with the medical aspects of death—all this will greatly influence the quality of life still remaining.

Chapter 6

YOUR FUNERAL PLANS

Beware of Vultures

Remember that warm, lovable movie about the cute little girl and her even cuter daddy who went around selling worthless Bibles to little old ladies recently widowed? The scam was to pretend that the widow's deceased husband had ordered the Bible before dying. Of course, the grieving, bereaved spouse would want to pay the bill now.

There are a lot of "cute" vultures in real life hovering over those who have recently lost someone. Their favorite ploy is either to collect a nonexistent debt owed by the deceased or to deliver merchandise never ordered.

Another gimmick is to pretend that a phony life insurance policy needs one more premium payment before benefits come pouring in. There are lots of variations on this theme.

Widows are prime targets for bad investment schemes. Even bona fide investment firms will sometimes recommend changing stock portfolios merely to collect the commissions involved.

The moral is obvious: Be careful, go slow—and don't get your advice over cocktails, coffee, or the back fence.

Vultures come in all sizes.

The Bank as Executor

You are probably already using a bank for your commercial and savings accounts, investments or loans, and perhaps even a safe-deposit box.

You may want to look into some of the other ways your bank can help you set your house and your estate in order. There are bank specialists who can: prepare and execute your will; handle any trust fund; analyze your present estate for maximum future benefit to your family.

Naming a bank to serve as executor and trustee has many obvious advantages. You are served by a full-time staff with experience in the many complicated duties and procedures required to settle an estate. The bank's investment specialists can make decisions regarding the sale of securities or investments in order to meet cash requirements; this can mean a saving of thousands of dollars for the estate. These same qualified experts provide trust fund management that will best conserve principal and earn investment income. It is unreasonable to expect any individual executor or trustee to make investment decisions with the skill of men who spend their lifetimes doing precisely this type of work. Similarly, bank real estate and tax experts safeguard the interest of your beneficiaries.

The commission for executing an estate is the same—it is regulated by law—whether it is done by a bank or by an individual. The complicated duties of estate administration call for immediate and concerted attention; an inexperienced individual executor may be forced to engage professional assistance. Thus, the attempt to "keep the fee in the family" may often backfire.

Think Ahead

The emergency room at our local hospital has some strange cases. But the strangest I've run across was the woman who bathed her beloved poodle and then wanted to "finish" him with a nice fluffy dry coat. So she put the dog in the microwave oven in her kitchen. When she turned the oven on, the poor pooch blew apart into about a hundred pieces. The poor woman suffered a heart attack and arrived in the emergency room DOA.

The best laid plans of mice and men—as Robert Burns and John Steinbeck have reminded us—often go astray. We need to think ahead! What are the potential consequences of our actions?

For example, there are eleven million teen-agers in the United States between the ages of fifteen and nineteen. Last year one million of them became pregnant. Three hundred thousand had their babies aborted. Two hundred thousand entered hasty marriages—we used to call them "shotgun" weddings; they are usually about as lethal! They didn't think ahead.

How often do we do or say something without fully considering the possible effects. We regret it later, saying "I wish I hadn't done that!"

It isn't enough to live for the moment. The ripple effect applies to everything we do.

Please think ahead.

Prearranging Your Funeral

To assure that your "rites of passage" conform to your personal beliefs and do not become a financial burden for those who survive you, you may want to consider making arrangements and paying for your funeral now.

Remember that your funeral, although yours, also belongs to those who survive. Include them in your plans and wishes so that they will know what you want and will not be mere passive grief- (even guilt-) stricken spectators.

No one should waste money that is needed by the living, but a couple of thousand dollars to celebrate the life and death of a loved one doesn't seem inappropriate in an age of five-to-ten-thousand-dollar automobiles and wedding receptions. I don't think money should ever be allowed to assume top priority.

Careful counseling, at no charge, with a trusted funeral director can help avoid unwise planning or even fraudulent schemes involving the prefinancing of a specific funeral. All funeral homes have a prearrangement agreement form: You can keep your copy tucked right here in this book—the funeral director keeps his copy on file. Cemetery and crematorium directors have similar pre-need plans. Check with them now as well.

Souls on Ice

Cryogenic interment is a process whereby the body is frozen immediately after death in the hope that science will eventually find a cure for all terminal illnesses. It is also a deterrent to the process of aging; eventually the body can be thawed out and brought back to life.

Costing from twenty-five to fifty thousand dollars, this procedure strikes me as a rather expensive, wishful version of the Rip Van Winkle fable.

Besides, I'm not so sure I would want to wake up in some strange new world and culture—with all my friends and family gone.

I suppose I could sit around and tell anyone willing to listen about the good old days.

But, basically, it seems to me to be an uncreative approach to the natural law, a rather obstinate unwillingness to accept death, and another example of our desperate struggle to live forever.

The resurrection Christ promises us is so much safer, surer—and less expensive—than souls on ice.

Prefinancing Your Funeral

Planning and paying ahead will ensure that money will be available for your funeral and burial expenses. Moreover, family members won't have to make decisions under stress. Funeral homes and cemeteries offer several plans that allow you to make arrangements and pay for them in advance (e.g., through trusts, insurance policies, or debenture plans). When choosing any plan, be certain of its provisions and restrictions.

· *Trustee.* The law in most states requires that all monies paid to funeral directors for pre-need funeral plans be placed in trust. Upon receiving proof of death and the fact that the funeral services were performed, the trust's proceeds are paid to the funeral director.

· *Bank accounts.* You can set up a checking, savings, or trust account with three trustees: yourself, the funeral director, and a third party. Upon receiving a certified copy of a death certificate and a signature of two out of three trustees, the bank will pay the funeral director.

· *Insurance policies.* Many funeral establishments work together with insurance companies to provide insurance for pre-need planning. The funeral director is usually the designated beneficiary. However, you can name the beneficiary of your choice or make any changes you desire.

· *Debenture plans.* Some funeral directors offer a debenture payable at time of death. Basically, a debenture is similar to an unsecured note in that you give the funeral director money and you receive a written promise that the money will be held until the time of your death, when it will be used for funeral expenses.

Chapter 7

YOUR FUNERAL SERVICE

In Touch with Death

Clearly, Americans are getting back in touch with death. For many years we have relegated death to professionals. From medical care to religious needs, from wake to funeral and burial, the doctor, nurse, lawyer, policeman, fireman, minister, priest, rabbi, mortician, embalmer, cemetery director, and grave digger all handled death for us for a fee.

Today, more and more Americans have a greater awareness and are taking death back into their own hands. They are planning for, and participating in, the dying process: facing their own death more openly; taking an active part in the wake or funeral of someone close; forming church or memorial societies for simple burial or cremation; creating small community cemeteries; donating all or parts of their bodies for transplants or research; telling the truth to someone who is dying; using video cassettes or sound tapes to leave a personal "media" memorial; building their own coffins; joining groups like "Hospice" and "Shanti" to help others approach death with dignity and love; and reading about, watching, listening to, and discussing death as they have never done before.

Some Americans (such as yourself) are even reading books like *Set Your House in Order* and are preparing themselves in a realistic and practical way for death. Of course, the better we handle death, the better we will also get at living.

Planning Your Funeral and Memorial Services

A funeral service is a worship ritual performed with the body physically present, immediately before burial (interment) or cremation. A memorial service is a worship ritual held to memorialize the dead person with the body not present.

Christian funeral tradition usually includes four events or stages:

1. Private visits to the family home or funeral parlor, where the body is kept in a closed or open casket;
2. Public wake for all friends of the deceased—usually held in church or a funeral home—with a closed or open casket;
3. Religious funeral service, usually held in church and followed immediately by the procession to the cemetery;
4. Committal service, held in a cemetery chapel or at the graveside.

Practice Dying

An old story relates that in the year 348 B.C. the eighty-year-old Plato was asked, on his deathbed, if he would summarize his dialogues. Most of his thought, of course, has come down to us in the form of twenty-two philosophical debates or dialogues, usually with his old professor, Socrates, as interlocutor.

Plato was a great visionary and believed that truth could come only in those almost mystical moments of enlightenment. He recognized the spiritual soul as the life principle temporarily contained by the physical vehicle of a body.

Plato logically saw death as liberation, awakening, and remembering. The separated soul could now reason even more clearly and recognize the true nature of beings more readily. According to Plato, soon after death the soul would experience "judgment," in which a divine being would place before us all things, good and bad, from our lives and force us to face them.

Little wonder that when his friend asked him to sum up his life's work in one statement, wise old Plato responded: "Practice dying."

Your Funeral Service (cont'd)

Both funeral and memorial services are intended to fill the same need: to remember the deceased with respect (we "pay our respects") and to support the family with our friendship and solidarity in their moment of loss and need. Christians add the extra dimension of prayer and faith in God, in the Resurrection, and in the continuity of life everlasting.

Services vary greatly from place to place, from culture to culture, and from one faith to another. It is virtually impossible to outline one particular format. Nevertheless, in order to encourage you to think and plan ahead, a few suggestions may be helpful.

Again, please begin by calling your local priest or minister and make an appointment to sit down in your home or at the church or synagogue and outline your service. No one will consider this strange or premature. In fact, every minister appreciates the opportunity to offer counsel on death preparation. When you can talk about dying, you can talk about anything.

First, you might begin by planning your wake service. What used to be a real family affair in the home has become a bit formal in the mortuary setting, although it is sometimes convenient to have professionals handle the arrangements and some of the hospitality surrounding the wake. Because people have no idea how to behave when surrounded by death, it will take some imaginative preparation on the part of both church and mortuary staff to create a family celebration (cf. Planning Your Wake, pp. 89–91).

No Excuse Sunday

To make it possible for everyone to attend church next Sunday, we are going to have a special "No Excuse Sunday."

Cots will be placed in the vestibule for those who say, "Sunday is my only day to sleep." We will have steel helmets for those who say, "The roof would cave in if I ever came back to church." Blankets will be furnished for those who think the church is too cold; fans will be provided for those who say it's too hot.

We will have hearing aids for those who say the pastor speaks too softly, and cotton for those who say he preaches too loudly. Score cards will be available for those who like to list all the hypocrites.

A few floating unattached relatives will be in attendance for those who like to visit on Sundays. One entire section will be landscaped with real shrubbery and astro turf for those who find God in nature on Sunday mornings.

Finally, the sanctuary will be decorated with both Christmas poinsettias and Easter lilies for those who have never seen the church without them.

It's No Excuse Sunday! See you in church!

Your Funeral Service (cont'd)

Most people emphasize reception of family and friends at home (yours or the house of a close family member) two or three days before the funeral itself, as well as before and after the wake service.

Increasing numbers of people are planning their wakes in a church, often in conjunction with the funeral rites or Mass of Christian Burial, on the evening before the burial. This seems to be a much better time and place. It is easier for most people to attend, a better place and setting for celebration, and ideal for spilling over into a quiet, comfortable post-service reception, usually at home. Procession to the cemetery and burial rites then take place for the immediate family the following morning.

The pastor you consult will have many specific suggestions concerning the actual funeral service.

Catholics, Episcopalians, and some Protestants make wonderful use of white vestments for the priest and pall covering the casket (and other signs of hope), the Easter candle (symbol for the risen Lord, light of the world), holy water (reminder of baptismal promises), incense (like ascending prayers), the crucifix (symbol of love), and so forth.

Success

Facing death forces us to ask important questions about the meaning of life. What makes a life meaningful, valuable, or successful? What is success? What do philosophers, artists, athletes, and entertainers say it is? What do you say it is?

Here's what one person says success is:

To laugh often and love much; to win the respect of intelligent persons and the affection of children; to earn the approbation of honest critics and endure the betrayal of false friends; to appreciate beauty; to find the best in others; to give of oneself; to leave the world a little bit better, whether in the form of a healthy child, a garden patch, or an improved social condition; to have played and laughed with exultation; to know even one life has breathed easier because you have lived—this is to have succeeded.

In order to have succeeded, I personally would also need to believe, to let go, to dream a little, and to find a bit of peace. What is success for you? How are you going about achieving it? Create a checklist for yourself—and check it out. Here's to real, lasting success!

Your Funeral Service (cont'd)

Protestants use music effectively—solo, choral, communal —and often are more comfortable with participated prayers, spontaneous witness, and other forms of liturgical involvement by family and friends.

In any case, it will be immensely helpful to whoever leads your funeral rites to have your suggestions.

· I wish to have my wake/funeral services conducted at:

( ) Church _____

( ) Funeral home _____

( ) Other _____

· I wish the following person(s) to conduct my wake/ funeral service:

(1st choice) _____

(2nd choice) _____

· I wish the following person to give my eulogy:

(1st choice) _____

(2nd choice) _____

· Possibility of personalized, mimeographed booklets for all: _____

· Your favorite scripture readings: _____
_____

· Passages: _____

· Readers: _____

Help Wanted

Recently I was privileged to offer the Mass of the Angels for a little three-month-old baby who had died. Just before mass, the baby's father came up to me and handed me a love letter written by the mother to her little daughter so I could work it into the blessings. It was the perfect personal touch that our faith celebration needed to add human warmth to family loss.

These loving parents reminded me of a want ad I saw recently:

HELP WANTED—FULL-TIME JOB

HOURS: 24 hours a day, 365 days a year, for a minimum of 18 years. No time off for weekends or holidays. You cannot quit.

DUTIES: Assume all physical, moral, and financial responsibilities for another human being.

QUALIFICATIONS: Patience, compassion, understanding, and mature judgment.

SALARY: None. In fact, you must plan on spending at least $3,500 a year for the privilege of taking this job.

Incidentally, it's the most important job in the whole world. Strangely enough, it's the only profession you don't need a license to practice.

The job, of course, is parenthood.

Please don't apply until you're ready.

86

Your Funeral Service (cont'd)

· Spirit of homily or sermon: _____

· Individually composed intercessions or testimonials: _____

_____

· Offering procession or personal witness: _____

_____

· Appropriate hymns and music (and musicians): _____

_____

· Other (e.g., some services have made effective use of slides, tapes, recordings, etc.): _____

_____

_____

These are only highlights. Don't be dismayed by the number of options. Your pastor will be pleased to guide you on this most important journey.

The person you have designated to plan your funeral (see p. 17) will see to it that the person who leads your funeral service has access to this book, especially this chapter and the section entitled "Outline for Your Autobiography."

Are You God?

Recently I attended a moving funeral for a young Philippino woman who had died suddenly, leaving a husband and five young children. As I entered the mortuary for the wake service, her husband greeted me with a tearful mixture of courage and desperation: "Father, I don't know what I will do—our few friends in this country were *her* relatives and I'll never be able to raise the kids alone."

He led me up to the closed casket and introduced me to the children. They, too, were crying—but the older ones held small albums of family photos that showed their mother alive and smiling. They shared the pictures with everyone who came up to pay their respects and offer a prayer. It gave everyone something meaningful to do. Best of all, it said to all of us, "This is our mom, this is the way we will remember her, alive and smiling."

I led them all in prayers and then told them the good news, as I always try to do at funeral parlors, about flowers and faith, Easter and hope. Afterwards, as I was leaving, the smallest child, the four-year-old son, followed me to the mortuary door and, when we were all alone, tugged at my black cassock and asked hesitantly, "Are you God?" "No," I replied. "Your mommy is with God." "But I want her here with me. I miss her." Just then his older sister came up and asked, "What are we going to do with mommy tomorrow?" This gave me a chance to explain about the funeral mass and burial and why it's good for children and priests to cry once in a while.

Planning Your Wake

What happens between your death and your final service and burial is generally called the wake. It used to take place at home during the two to three days the family needed to build a casket, dig a grave, and so forth. This time gave everyone a chance to visit, "pay their respects," and offer support and solace to the bereaved family. Now a wake usually refers to the memorial service held the day before the body is buried or (if the body is cremated) a few days after death, allowing time to contact people.

There are so many alternatives today for all faiths that the most sensible approach is to make an appointment with your pastor. Discuss what kind of wake and memorial service you would like.

The wake or public mourning can be held with or without the body, in the home, mortuary, or church. It gives everyone a chance to reflect quietly on the meaning of your life and death to them. It might include some readings, prayers, or even a song and just plain silence.

Catholics often include the rosary, a meditative repetition of Our Fathers and Hail Marys, which focus faith on the life, death, and resurrection of Christ. Even more effective are the scriptural wake services, which combine God's word with the people's response. There are many little booklets available as outline guides.

The most meaningful wakes I have attended gave people a chance to share a personal memory or two. Once an uncle played his niece's favorite song on the guitar. Another time a daughter read a letter to her dead father.

(continued)

"Crazy California"

I was born and grew up in South Bend, Indiana. So I really shouldn't be defensive. But it bothers me when I hear people talk about "crazy California"—as if we had cornered the market on kooks! Perhaps the West Coast is simply more liberating—or searching more desperately.

In any case, we certainly are into rentals. We have rent-an-everything: cars, condominiums, crutches, costumes, tuxedos, trailers, furniture, party supplies (including your date!)—ranging from the most absurd ("Rent-a-Wife") to the most practical ("Rent-a-Casket").

First a word about "Rent-a-Wife." The following sad ad, which recently appeared in our newspapers, says it all: "Rent-a-Wife will give your dinner parties; build your bookshelves; shop for presents, food, and clothes; decorate; pay your bills; jump out of a cake; do your errands; care for your home while you are away; take your relatives on tour; arrange your vacation—all for $50 per service." Sounds like the newest version of the oldest profession.

On the other hand, "Rent-a-Casket" is a wonderfully creative idea developed by one of our San Francisco Bay Area funeral directors as an alternative to the high cost of dying.

For less than $250, you can rent a beautiful $1,500 metal or oak coffin that is bottomless and slips over the inexpensive particleboard box. It is removed after the service for simple burial, interment, or cremation.

You can have it both ways: the external appearance of baronial splendor and ageless solidity and the true simplicity of a "make-your-own" coffin that points to passage.

So maybe crazy California isn't so crazy, after all!

90

Your Wake (cont'd)

Often, if a few members of the family begin by expressing their love and appreciation, it permits others to voice their feelings of grief and gratitude—without the need for liquid courage. There will be tears as well as smiles, regret and hope. People will realize that wakes and funerals are not for the dead but for the living!

But you give the first sign by establishing, ahead of time, the spirit you want for your wake or memorial service. Talk it over with your minister and family. Make a few notes. The wake, like any ritual, needs a leader. The only reason wakes are often dry and strained is that no one really knows what to do, or what you wanted, or how best to commemorate your death.

Give them a little outline guide:

Favorite readings: ——————————————————

Special prayers: ——————————————————

Personal witness: ——————————————————

Possible musical selections: ——————————————

Open or closed coffin: —————————————————

Memorial gifts (instead of flowers) to: ——————

Type of memorial card preferred: ————————

My own personal contribution*: ——————————

* More and more people are writing, tape recording, or videotaping a memorial message that is often shared with everyone at the wake or funeral service. Think about it.

Some of My Best Friends

A good deal of pop literature seems bent on discrediting the funeral profession in America because of the unscrupulous commercial practices and dishonesty of a minority. God knows, our funeral directors have a problem. In the United States each year two million deaths are handled by twenty thousand morticians—giving each an average of only two funerals per week. But because a few mortuaries handle most of the funerals, the majority often average less than one funeral per week. And we know the abuses that can arise as a result: A manipulative mortician might use unctuous jargon to con the grief-stricken relatives making funeral arrangements (usually for the first time in their lives) into wasting money on lavish extras.

I have been stationed in large city parishes averaging up to three funerals per week and have worked with dozens of funeral directors over the past fifteen years. I have found only a handful who were the least bit offensive or unethical. They are easy to spot! They try too hard, drink too much, and are scared silly of competition. The fact is that the vast majority of morticians I know approach their profession as a vocation, a commitment to serve and assist with grace and graciousness. They are community-conscious leaders who know how to create a sense of community during life's loneliest moment. You can tell them by their compassion, candor, and sense of humor.

A priest who loses his temper in the confessional, a minister who creates public scandal, an evangelist who badgers his congregation for donations "for Christ's sake," a doctor who bilks welfare monies by falsifying his records, a lawyer who is motivated by profit rather than justice, a mortician who takes advantage of the bereaved—all are *un*professionals (to put it charitably) and are certainly the exceptions. Search a bit and you will always discover the good and honest people in this world who do care for you!

92

The Funeral Director

You should discuss any or all of these points with your funeral director:

Prefinancing? _____

Coffin or casket (type/cost) _____

Embalming (i.e., do you prefer open or closed casket?) __
_____

Transportation needs _____
_____

Flowers: yes _____ no _____ If you answered yes, how
do you want them disposed of after the funeral?
church _____ hospital _____ rest home _____ other _____

If you answered no, indicate an appropriate memorial or
charity to which gifts can be made. (This should be
included with your obituary notice.)

Other specifics:

_____

_____

_____

_____

_____

_____

Shanti

People who are dying—and are brave enough to face the fact—have lots of questions:

Why me? Why now?

How can I stand the pain?

I'm afraid. What can I do?

What's it like? Does it hurt to die?

What was the purpose of my life anyway?

Who will remember me? What will happen to my family?

Relatives and friends of the dying have their own questions:

What can I say to him?

Will talking about illness and the possibility of death make the patient depressed?

Why do I feel so guilty?

What can I do?

What will I do without her?

No one has all the answers. Death, like life, is a mystery. But beautiful groups of volunteers like "Shanti Project" can help others face death, ask the questions, and sometimes find their own answers.

Shanti is a Sanskrit word meaning "inner peace." The Shanti Project offers caring, counseling, and emotional support for patients and families facing life-threatening illnesses. Their simple presence and sharing relieves some of the fears of isolation, frustration, and depression.

The Shanti Project is based in Berkeley, California, a location apparently created by God for experimentation and pilot projects.

But the spirit of Shanti is located in the hearts of generous, caring people everywhere—just waiting to be turned on and organized.

Shanti be with you.

Memorial Societies

Funeral or memorial societies can be helpful in providing information for preplanning by putting you in touch with the mortuaries in your area that emphasize simplicity and economy. Some memorial societies, especially those sponsored by churches, are more than consumer organizations and offer both referrals for physical needs as well as a spiritual or religious sense of death.

Some funeral directors are shocked and enraged at the very mention of memorial societies. However, most morticians cooperate wisely and willingly, knowing that the memorial society will eventually use their services—and that good mortuaries can beat the services and prices offered by the society.

Memorial Societies are only necessary when you cannot find a combination of mortuary/cemetery/crematorium that will meet your physical and spiritual needs.

Much of the motivation to put this guidebook together grew out of memorial society literature. But now that you have this little workbook and are doing your homework to prepare for your own death, you are really providing much of the society's service for yourself.

For additional information, including a complete list of memorial societies in the United States and Canada, write:

The Continental Association
  of Funeral and Memorial Societies
1828 L Street N.W.
Washington, D.C. 20036

Chapter 8

YOUR BURIAL
OR . . .

Suicide

Not long ago, a priest I had lived with and worked with for several years committed suicide by jumping off the Golden Gate Bridge. It was hushed up in the papers and news because "priests don't do that."

But priests are human beings just like you, equally susceptible to discouragement and despair. Sometimes it's just as hard to stay in love with or preserve hope in Jesus Christ as it is with any other person.

Nobody worries too much about sin in connection with suicide since people desperate enough to take their own lives seldom have clear knowledge or free will.

Still, the tragedy reminded me that too many people in our lonely, hung-up world are driven to the point of quick suicide with guns, pills, or desperate acts; or slow suicide with drugs, drinking, and smoking.

Which is more terrible: the hopeless sufferer who drives off a cliff or the helpless achiever who drives himself to an early grave for profit, prestige, or pleasure? Both are life-denying, senseless acts.

In fact, killing yourself slowly each day is a form of suicide that simply requires a little less character and appears a bit more respectable.

Obviously, what we all need is hope and dreams—a reason to live, to get up in the morning, an active trust in Our Father who is in Heaven.

Death Certificate

Although most of this information is already contained in your autobiographical description, this standard death certificate is included here as an illustrative example for your information.

CERTIFICATE OF DEATH	
STATE OF CALIFORNIA	

	STATE FILE NUMBER			LOCAL REGISTRATION DISTRICT AND CERTIFICATE NUMBER	
	1A. NAME OF DECEDENT—FIRST	1B. MIDDLE	1C. LAST	2A. DATE OF DEATH (MONTH, DAY, YEAR)	2B. HOUR
DECEDENT PERSONAL DATA	3. SEX	4. RACE	5. ETHNICITY	6. DATE OF BIRTH	7. AGE / IF UNDER 1 YEAR MONTHS DAYS / IF UNDER 24 HOURS HOURS MINUTES / YEARS
	8. BIRTHPLACE OF DECEDENT (STATE OR FOREIGN COUNTRY)	9. NAME AND BIRTHPLACE OF FATHER		10. BIRTH NAME AND BIRTHPLACE OF MOTHER	
	11. CITIZEN OF WHAT COUNTRY	12. SOCIAL SECURITY NUMBER	13. MARITAL STATUS	14. NAME OF SURVIVING SPOUSE (IF WIFE, ENTER BIRTH NAME)	
	15. PRIMARY OCCUPATION	16. NUMBER OF YEARS THIS OCCUPATION	17. EMPLOYER (IF SELF-EMPLOYED, SO STATE)	18. KIND OF INDUSTRY OR BUSINESS	
USUAL RESIDENCE	19A. USUAL RESIDENCE—STREET ADDRESS (STREET AND NUMBER OR LOCATION)		19B.	19C. CITY OR TOWN	
	19D. COUNTY		19E. STATE	20. NAME AND ADDRESS OF INFORMANT—RELATIONSHIP	
PLACE OF DEATH	21A. PLACE OF DEATH		21B. COUNTY		
	21C. STREET ADDRESS (STREET AND NUMBER OR LOCATION)		21D. CITY OR TOWN		
CAUSE OF DEATH	22. DEATH WAS CAUSED BY: (ENTER ONLY ONE CAUSE PER LINE FOR A, B AND C)			24. WAS DEATH REPORTED TO CORONER?	
	IMMEDIATE CAUSE (A)			APPROXIMATE INTERVAL BETWEEN ONSET AND DEATH	
	CONDITIONS, IF ANY, WHICH GAVE RISE TO THE IMMEDIATE CAUSE, STATING THE UNDERLYING CAUSE LAST,	DUE TO, OR AS A CONSEQUENCE OF (B)			25. WAS BIOPSY PERFORMED?
		DUE TO, OR AS A CONSEQUENCE OF (C)			26. WAS AUTOPSY PERFORMED?
	23. OTHER CONDITIONS CONTRIBUTING BUT NOT RELATED TO THE IMMEDIATE CAUSE OF DEATH		27. WAS OPERATION PERFORMED FOR ANY CONDITION IN ITEMS 22 OR 23? TYPE OF OPERATION DATE		
PHYSICIAN'S CERTIFICATION	28A. I CERTIFY THAT DEATH OCCURRED AT THE HOUR, DATE AND PLACE STATED FROM THE CAUSES STATED. I ATTENDED DECEDENT SINCE (ENTER MO, DA, YR.) I LAST SAW DECEDENT ALIVE (ENTER MO, DA, YR.)	28B. PHYSICIAN—SIGNATURE AND DEGREE OR TITLE		28C. DATE SIGNED	28D. PHYSICIAN'S LICENSE NUMBER
		28E. TYPE PHYSICIAN'S NAME AND ADDRESS			
INJURY INFORMATION	29. SPECIFY ACCIDENT, SUICIDE, ETC.	30. PLACE OF INJURY		31. INJURY AT WORK	32A. DATE OF INJURY—MONTH, DAY, YEAR	32B. HOUR
	33. LOCATION (STREET AND NUMBER OR LOCATION AND CITY OR TOWN)		34. DESCRIBE HOW INJURY OCCURRED (EVENTS WHICH RESULTED IN INJURY)		
CORONER'S USE ONLY	35A. I CERTIFY THAT DEATH OCCURRED AT THE HOUR, DATE AND PLACE STATED FROM THE CAUSES STATED, AS REQUIRED BY LAW I HAVE HELD AN (INQUEST—INVESTIGATION)	35B. CORONER—SIGNATURE AND DEGREE OR TITLE			35C. DATE SIGNED
	36. DISPOSITION	37. DATE—MONTH, DAY, YEAR	38. NAME AND ADDRESS OF CEMETERY OR CREMATORY	39. EMBALMER'S LICENSE NUMBER AND SIGNATURE	
	40. NAME OF FUNERAL DIRECTOR (OR PERSON ACTING AS SUCH)	41. LOCAL REGISTRAR—SIGNATURE		42. DATE ACCEPTED BY LOCAL REGISTRAR	
STATE REGISTRAR	A.	B.	C.	D.	E.	F.

VS-11 (5-78)

Please Bury Your Dead

My cousin plays with a rock band called Chicago. One member of the group died recently, tragically, mysteriously. Weeks after the funeral and burial, the other members of the band still couldn't accept his passing. "We don't want to let him go!" they told me.

It is amazing how many people simply refuse to accept the painful reality of death! The widow who continues to set a place at the table for the husband who's gone; the empty crib that becomes a shrine to fantasy; the dangerously stoic young man ("Isn't he brave!") who handles his parent's death with surface calm.

We all tend to hide our deepest feelings from others. We think that whatever makes us feel bad is somehow evil. We avoid the hard, hurting work of mourning, that gradual breaking of countless small memories that are ingrained in our psyches. As a result, there are dead people still running around loose and causing all sorts of trouble.

Until we face facts, begin to let go, and buckle down to the extremely difficult, unpleasant work of mourning, neither the dead nor we will find peace.

My dear, suffering friend: Please bury your dead.

Obituary Notice

Here is an opportunity to complete your own obituary notice for the newspaper. It will allow you to include more than just the bare facts.

Name, age, place of birth _____

_____

Occupation _____

Education _____

Membership(s) _____

Military service _____

Outstanding achievements _____

_____

_____

Immediate family _____

_____

_____

P.S. Once, when my family and I had just read the obituary notice (sometimes teasingly referred to as the "Irish Sports Page") of a dear friend, I asked my mom and dad how they would want their obituaries to read. We had a long, fascinating discussion of values, real accomplishments, and the meaning of life, faith, and the family. Writing your own brief death notice will hopefully give you and your family the opportunity to share a similar experience. Another revealing exercise might be to write your own epitaph: What would you want inscribed on your tombstone (assuming you have one)?

_____

_____

Coffins for Christmas

I am already planning my gifts for next Christmas—and have I got a great idea for my family: coffins!

Wait a minute! I can see the expression on your face. Go ahead, smile and giggle if you must. I'm "live" serious!

I've found a Coffin Company (P. O. Box 6690, Stanford, Cal. 94305) that has simple, attractive coffins for about thirty dollars each. Constructed of sturdy fiberboard, they are easy to stash away or store things in. The soft white exterior surface can be painted, decorated, or left as is. They will make good gifts and great conversation pieces.

Best of all, you can personalize these simple, natural coffins with six rope handles—and live with it. For example, add a couple of shelves and, presto, you have a bookcase or wine bottle rack; placed under the window it becomes a hope chest; next to a couch it's transformed into a coffee table. In fact, if you're good with your hands and can do a little light carpentry, just write the Coffin Company for a set of plans (for two or three dollars) and make your own!

Like the old man who asked that the wood from the family dining room table be used to make his coffin, buying or building your own simple coffin well in advance allows you to live comfortably with the reality of death and preserve some marvelous memories of your own.

Coffins for Christmas . . . or Easter!

Burial

The fact that burial plots are usually available only in twos (like bunk beds) may reflect the human instinct to be buried—as we live—in community. Cemeteries can be familial, religious, ethnic, military, fraternal, no matter, there is almost always a sense of community. A cemetery is also primarily a place for the living. This is made beautifully apparent on Easter, Father's Day, Mother's Day, or Memorial Day—especially in Catholic cemeteries, where you always see family members returning to pray, remember, and reinforce their faith in the Resurrection. It is interesting that we had cemeteries (or catacombs) even before we had churches. They were the first churches.

It is difficult to generalize about burial costs, options, and requirements. Here are a few very rough estimates for various alternatives:

Plot (ground)	$350–$400
Burial (wall liner, labor, etc.)	$750–$800
Crypt (above ground): mausoleum	$900–$2500
garden	$700–$2000

Whatever you decide, be sure to arrange for this well ahead of time. "Shopping around" after death becomes a terrible—sometimes impossible—burden for survivors. Read on to page 105 and fill out your burial wishes:

Catacomb Cemeteries

Among the warmest memories of my life are the first six months after my ordination in Rome in 1963. At least once a week several of us young priests would make an early morning minipilgrimage of faith down into the literally miles of catacombs interwoven around and under the Eternal City.

Like miners exploring for buried treasure, we would invade the cool darkness in a candlelight procession—carrying bread, wine, vestments, and missals—to discover a suitable place to express our belief in the risen Lord.

As we passed along the narrow, labyrinthian corridors, we would pause to read the inscriptions on the burial niches of our earliest Christian ancestors, the first martyrs —the Church before there were churches—who were forced to live and die for their faith underground.

Every several hundred feet, the nineteen-hundred-year-old hallway would bubble out into a small cave-like room with a tomb-table in the middle. This became our altar, our chapel for a mass celebration of life's Easter Mysteries of death and the Resurrection.

Today's cemeteries and churches are at ground level. But whenever I visit a grave or drive by those long, symmetrical burial markers off the freeway, I still see the Christian catacombs of courage and celebration—and remember that cemeteries are for the living.

Cemetery

Name of cemetery or crematorium ⎯⎯⎯⎯⎯⎯⎯

Address ⎯⎯⎯⎯⎯⎯⎯ City ⎯⎯⎯⎯⎯⎯⎯

Location of family burial estate ⎯⎯⎯⎯⎯⎯⎯

Block ⎯⎯ Section ⎯⎯ Lot ⎯⎯ Grave nos. ⎯⎯

Lot owner's name ⎯⎯⎯⎯⎯ Address ⎯⎯⎯⎯⎯

Co-owner's name ⎯⎯⎯⎯⎯ Address ⎯⎯⎯⎯⎯

Location of deed ⎯⎯⎯⎯⎯⎯⎯⎯⎯⎯⎯

Assignments of spaces in family burial estate:

1. Lot No. ⎯⎯ Graves ⎯⎯ for ⎯⎯⎯⎯⎯
   name

2. Lot No. ⎯⎯ Graves ⎯⎯ for ⎯⎯⎯⎯⎯
   name

3. Lot No. ⎯⎯ Graves ⎯⎯ for ⎯⎯⎯⎯⎯
   name

4. Lot No. ⎯⎯ Graves ⎯⎯ for ⎯⎯⎯⎯⎯

Here are some advantages in selecting your burial estate now:

1. You can choose your estate calmly, thoughtfully, together with others.
2. When you select in advance, you have the advantage of low prices in predeveloped sections.
3. You can usually pay on easy credit terms spread out over a period of years.
4. You get choice locations.
5. You will have time to consider the reliability of the memorial park or cemetery of your choice, as well as such features as perpetual care, insured payments, less expensive memorials, and special services.

Sunlight

Unfortunately, the very thought or mention of cremation generates more heat than light. Cremation is an ancient practice, recorded in Greece as early as 1000 B.C. Our modern form of cremation, however, only began in 1869, when the Italian scientist Ludovico Brunetti invented the crematorium.

An International Medical Congress in Florence held that same year urged all nations to promote cremation "as an aid to public health and to save the land for the living."

The process is very simple. The dead body is received in the crematorium chapel. The casket is placed on a catafalque. The pallbearers stand to either side while the usual service for the dead is conducted. At the words "ashes to ashes, dust to dust," the casket is lowered below floor level, leaving only the flowers visible.

After family and friends have left, the casket is lowered into the retort, a long, white-tiled chamber, and the doors are electrically sealed for four hours while fire consumes all but the bones.

Later the bones are reduced and packed, together with the ashes, in a little square box about the size of a shoe box, usually weighing no more than six to eight pounds. This box is returned to the family for disposition in a cemetery, columbarium, or at home.

Some consider cremation a barbaric bonfire, others as a purifying light like the sun. I think of cremation as accomplishing in hours what would otherwise take years.

Since I plan to leave my body to medical science, that light doesn't scare me at all.

Cremation

In 1886 the Church forbade cremation for Catholics. It did not condemn cremation itself; rather, it objected to the denial of the Christian belief in the Resurrection of the dead and the immortality of the soul.

In 1963 the Catholic church—recognizing valid personal and hygienic reasons for cremation as well as occasional spatial or economic problems implicit in regular burial—removed the ban on cremation for Catholics, thereby permitting full funeral rites even with the body or remains present. Nevertheless, it continued to prefer the traditional wake service, funeral mass, and burial in the consecrated ground of a Catholic cemetery (which, despite uninformed rumors to the contrary, often operates at a loss—just as Catholic schools and hospitals do!).

As a result of this seventy-five-year ban by the Catholic church—and the resistance to cremation by such other religious groups as the Jews—cremation is still far from popular. The cremation rate for 1976 was slightly less than 10 per cent of the total deaths in Canada and the United States. (Most of those cremations took place in California, perhaps in part because of the lack of a sense of community and family roots.) By way of comparison, the cremation rate in Great Britain for 1976 was 62 per cent.

Hiding God

Once upon a time there were three wise men who were given the task of hiding God so well that no one would ever find him again. They all sat down at the council table to ponder the possibilities.

The first wise man suggested that God should be hidden on the farthest star. However, the second wise man feared that spaceships would one day reach that star and God would be discovered. He recommended that God be hidden at the bottom of the deepest ocean. But the third wise man said that some day food would be grown on the bottom of the ocean to feed our starving brothers and sisters in the Third World. They would eventually find God at the ocean's bottom.

The third wise man finally suggested that the only place to hide God so that no one would ever find him again would be inside a human person. No one would ever think of looking for God in an ordinary man or woman.

And that's precisely what happened.

Cremation (cont'd)

So that you can make your own personal choice, it is important to think of cremation as one type of preparation for memorialization that may (or may not) include the other steps in your rite of passage: wake, funeral or memorial service, and burial or interment.

Give your decision some thought and prayer. Talk to some trusted professionals and close friends. Review your options and consider the feelings of those who love you. Then indicate your choices below:

I would like my body cremated: yes ⎯ no ⎯

My remains (ashes) should be present at my funeral service: yes ⎯ no ⎯

My remains are to be disposed of:

- by means of burial at: ⎯⎯⎯⎯⎯⎯⎯⎯⎯⎯⎯⎯⎯

- by inurnment (in a small urn placed in a niche at a columbarium) at: ⎯⎯⎯⎯⎯⎯⎯⎯⎯⎯⎯⎯⎯

- by scattering or sprinkling (check local legal restrictions first) at: ⎯⎯⎯⎯⎯⎯⎯⎯⎯⎯⎯⎯⎯

No cremation shall take place until a written authority to cremate by the proper relative or legal representative of the deceased has been filed with the health office of this city.

The undersigned hereby requests and authorizes the ————————— Cemetery Association to cremate the remains of —————————————, who died at ——————————————— in the ——————— day of ——————— 19 ———————.

—————————————————————
Signature of relative or legal representative

—————————————————————
Address

—————————————————————
Relation to deceased or authority to sign

Funeral Director —————————————————————

110

Chapter 9

YOUR GIFT

Raison d'Être

Yesterday afternoon I was on the roof of the center where I work organizing a massive pile of notes. A wild wind kept whipping at the files and folders on my lap. I couldn't help noticing how hard it is to write on a moving planet. I wrote slowly because I know you don't read too fast.

Suddenly I was overcome by the most outrageous temptation: What would happen if I simply flung the whole mass (or mess) of folders/papers/ideas off the roof to the winds—like so many mini-kites or paper airplane confetti. All that work! All those precious notes! Would my life come unglued? Would my world fall apart? It was a great example or reminder of how much importance we place in *things*.

It is said that the fate of people in concentration camps was decided in the first three weeks. Could they handle being stripped of everything—and still have themselves, their values, their hopes and dreams? That is, when they suddenly found themselves with nothing, would they still have something to live for?

Would you?

Giving Yourself Away

The chapter may frighten you if you are not comfortable with the fact that you really are going to die someday. Perhaps you should read it later. Wait until you are in a charitable, loving mood to read it and act on it.

You may be amazed to learn that you can give part or all of yourself away after you die to ensure the health and life of others. You can do this without violating your religious beliefs and without any irreverence to your body. You can make this beautiful contribution and still have a conventional funeral and burial. All you need is a little information and advance planning.

This gift of yourself is called an anatomical gift. There are many anatomical gifts you can make at the time of your death. You can donate your:

> • *corneas* (the clear window in the front of your eyes): Transplantation of the cornea has been done successfully for several decades. Demand far exceeds supply. There are over fifty eye banks in the United States.
> • *eardrum* and *three small middle bones:* These can be transplanted into the middle ear of those who have lost these bones (and consequently their hearing) through disease, injury, or birth defects.
> • *bone and cartilage:* These may be taken from several different parts of your body to repair bony defects.

Charlie

I'm very proud of an old (well, not so very old) seminary classmate of mine. His name is Charlie. He's a great basketball player and has a great sense of humor. He occasionally smokes a cigar. Charlie has a marvelous memory and is always busy helping someone. He is a priest in New York City, rector of the Cathedral Seminary. My friend is a compassionate, gentle man.

Charlie was in the national news recently. He was at St. Luke's Hospital in New York City counseling a family whose fifteen-year-old son had just been shot by a thirteen-year-old boy from Harlem. With Charlie's support, the parents of that fifteen-year-old boy, lying there in a coma like a vegetable, did two heroic things.

First of all, after praying for twenty-four hours for some miracle to heal their boy, they allowed the doctors to disconnect one respirator (which permitted their son to die) and plug in another kind (which would keep his organs alive for donation purposes). Second, at a time when friends and families of murder victims are calling for the restoration of the death penalty, these parents chose to follow Christ, turn the other cheek, and forgive their son's murderer.

I'm proud of Charlie. But Charlie must be much prouder of those Christian parents.

Giving Yourself Away (cont'd)

- *pituitary gland:* This gift supplies growth hormones to certain children who might not otherwise reach their natural height.
- *skin:* This is used for treatment of very severe burns; it can be preserved after removal from the body and used at a later date.
- *kidneys:* This successful and life-saving transplant operation has been performed since the mid-1950s; there are many more persons in need of kidneys than there are available organs.
- *heart:* Heart transplants have received the greatest amount of publicity. Some people fear that if they offer their hearts an overzealous heart surgeon will remove it before they are completely dead. But both the law and medical ethics require that donor organs may be removed only after your body and brain are certified legally dead.
- *entire body:* Check with your local state curator's office or medical school concerning forms to be filled out and conditions for acceptance.

Remember that advance planning is essential and that your gift of part or all of your body will be accepted only if it is really needed. If you decide to make such a gift, the important thing is to let people know. The best way is to obtain from your state curator's office or nearest transplant bank a Uniform Donor Card (I notice that some states are now making these available with auto-license renewals)— or use this one:

115

Practicing What We Preach

A friend wrote to me recently, asking when all of us evangelizing Christians were going to start practicing what we preach. To drive the point home, he quoted the following:

Listen, Christians:

I was hungry and you formed a humanities club and discussed my hunger.

I was imprisoned and you crept off quietly to your chapel in the cellar and prayed for my release.

I was naked and in your mind you debated the morality of my appearance.

I was sick and you knelt and thanked God for your health.

I was homeless and you preached to me of the spiritual shelter of the love of God.

I was lonely and you left me alone to pray for me.

You seem so holy, so close to God, but I'm still very hungry . . . and lonely . . . and cold.

It is a good reminder. In fact, it sounds rather familiar. We Christians are slowly hearing it changing gradually, and doing something about it . . .

I think . . . I hope.

Uniform Donor Card

Donor: _____

Print or type your name

In the hope that I may help others, I hereby make this anatomical gift, if medically accepted, to take effect after my death. The instructions below indicate my desire.

I give:　(a) _____ any needed organs or parts

　　　　　(b) _____ only the following organs or parts

_____

(Specify the organ(s) or part(s)

(or, for the purposes of transplantation and, consequently medical research or education):　(c) _____ my body, unembalmed and unautopsied, for anatomical study if needed

Limitation or special wishes, if any: _____
Signature of the donor and the following two witnesses in the presence of each other:

_____	_____
Your signature as donor	Date of birth
_____	_____
Date signed	City and state
_____	_____
Witness	Witness

This is a legal document under the Uniform Anatomical Gift Act (or similar laws).

For further information, consult your physician or write:
　　National Kidney Foundation
　　116 East 27 Street, New York, N.Y. 60016

List here your local transplant bank (for organs or parts):

_____

and your State Curator's Office (for whole-body gift):

_____

(Be sure to include address, phone (incl. weekend phone numbers) so that they can be notified immediately when you die.)

Hospice

They do what the church used to do before it got so big and busy. They do what the hospital used to do before it got so big and busy. They are called Hospice and they provide physical and emotional hospitality for those who are completing the journey of life.

The word "hospice" goes back to the Middle Ages when Christians set up "way stations" for needy travelers. The first modern hospice was founded in Dublin in the 1850s by the Irish Sisters of Charity. In 1905 St. Joseph's Hospice was built in London. In North America there are currently many hospices. (For a complete list, write: National Hospice Organization, 765 Prospect Street, New Haven, Conn. 06511.)

Trained hospice professionals visit the terminally ill in their homes and offer comfort, counseling, and pain control for the dying person and the family. Nursing services and therapists help them handle the reality of death and allow them to live life fully in familiar, loving family surroundings. A special medicinal drink called Brompton's mixture, containing alcohol and morphine, is scrupulously administered by a doctor to lessen pain while leaving the patient totally alert.

Hospice isn't about dying so much as living. It's about "there-ness" being there, and caring.

One volunteer nurse summed it up as follows: "Working with the dying gives me a greater reason for living. When I go home, I hug my kids, look at the birds, and appreciate things that I might not be as conscious of otherwise."

Other Gifts

Fill out your uniform donor card, have your two witnesses sign it together and make three copies:

1. one for your local transplant bank, which is

   _____.

2. one to be attached to your will (or this book)
3. one you should carry with you at all times (in your wallet or purse)

P.S. Medic-Alert (Turlock, Cal. 95380) will send you an identification bracelet or necklace engraved with personal health data (blood type, allergies, etc.) and donor information. There is a small fee, but this ID will save precious time and lives.

There are many things you can give to others after you die. These might include nonorganic materials such as *glasses* (mail to: New Eyes for the Needy, Inc., Short Hill, N.J. 07078); *pills:* if fairly fresh and clean, they can be used legally by missionaries outside the United States and Canada (send to: Human Resource Center, 2 W. Olive Ave., Redlands, Ca. 92373); *gold fillings* (send to: School of Dentistry, University of Southern California, Los Angeles, Cal. 90007).

There are, of course, many ways to give yourself *before* you die:

Your time: Volunteer for health or community-service work.

Your blood: Call the American Red Cross or local blood bank.

Yourself: Agree to serve as a research subject; call the nearest institute for medical research or medical school.

Chapter 10

GUIDES

Affirmation

A lot of people think self-fulfillment comes from self-indulgence. But fulfillment, strange as it may seem, is not something you can give yourself. Contrary to a lot of human-potential cliches, you don't will fulfillment into being through the power of positive thinking.

Fulfillment comes through affirmation. And affirmation is something given to you by others and, of course, something you can give. To be affirmed is to receive the gift of yourself from another person. To affirm another is to become a co-creator, together with God, of that person.

Zippy commercials tell us that you only go around this world once, so grab all you can. Self-help best-sellers tell us to look out for Number One, win through intimidation, and eradicate your erroneous zones.

They're all right about the need to love yourself first before you can love another person or God. But they forget to mention that we all learn to love ourselves by being *loved* by someone else. Love, affirmation, and fulfillment are therefore gifts given to us by someone else, precious gifts we can give back in return.

That kind of changes the whole picture.

Guide for Your Executor

The Executor of your estate has a difficult job. You may select anyone you wish, including your wife or a member of your family, as executor. However, in view of the importance of a wise, competent executor for the family's future welfare, many people prefer to name a bank. To help you decide just who might be the best choice in your case, here is a list of the principal duties of an executor:

1. Obtain original of last will. If it is kept in a safe-deposit box, it is sometimes necessary to obtain a court order to open same.
2. Offer the will, through an attorney, for probate in court.
3. Prove execution of the will in court through the subscribing witnesses or by some other means.
4. Secure letters testamentary from the court; these are the executor's legal authority to administer and settle the estate.
5. Secure appointment from the court and furnish required bond (unless otherwise stipulated in the will).
6. Notify all persons interested in the estate of the status of the deceased; this includes creditors, bank, safe-deposit companies, insurance companies, and the post office, among others.
7. Take possession of all property of the deceased.
8. Prepare a detailed inventory of all assets and liabilities; keep an accurate record of all stocks, bonds, mortgages, notes, and watch investments for bond calls, interest deposits, stock rights, etc.

(continued)

Remember When

Remember when you could convert ashcan covers into Roman shields, oatmeal boxes into telephones, bottle tops into checkers, broomsticks into baseball bats, discarded mattresses into trampolines, umbrella ribs into bows and arrows, candlesticks into trumpets, orange crates into store counters, peanut shells into earrings, hatboxes into drums, clothespins into pistols, and lumps of sugar into dice?

You also qualify if you can remember resharpening old razor blades by honing them against the inside of a drinking glass or making a racing car out of a wooden box, a plank, and abandoned baby-carriage wheels.

Do you recall playing games that required only one player, games that were I.Q.-less and scoreless, but not pointless or joyless—games like looking at clouds to see faces, castles, animals, angels, and God; or closing your eyes and holding your breath in front of a mirror to see how you would look if you were dead?

If you can remember any of these things and smile a little, you're not dead yet!

Guide for Your Executor (cont'd)

9. File inventory and appraisal in court.
10. Attend meetings of appraisers; protect property by means of insurance.
11. Obtain all property in custody of others; pay all debts and secure release of any property held as collateral for loans, etc.
12. Obtain order to advertise for claims against the estate and arrange for such ads.
13. If circumstances require sale of property, have property listed and negotiate sale.
14. Dispose of property as required by will or, if not specified, determine disposition.
15. Prepare and file all income tax returns, federal, state, and estate tax returns when necessary.
16. Get final release from all legatees when legacies are paid.

Christian Crutch

The Reverend William Sloane Coffin, chaplain at Yale, speaking at an anti-Vietnam war rally, was asked by one of the students, "How can you believe in that Christian nonsense? Don't you know it's just a crutch!"

Chaplain Coffin stopped and reflected for a moment and then answered his heckler, "What makes you think you don't limp?"

I recently told this story to a friend of mine, to encourage him to rely on his faith, his Christian center, God's grace gift of hope, to discover true peace in his life. His response to me was, "Heck, I'm not embarrassed to use a crutch. But what I need is a wheelchair!"

There are times when some of us could use a stretcher—or an ambulance!

So God's grace is a crutch. So what? So a Christ-like faith in something more and something greater is a wheelchair. So what? So the Bible is a stretcher. So what? So the sacraments, prayer, and worship in community are an ambulance? So what?

So who doesn't need a lift now and again?

Guide for the Arranger of Your Funeral

This chronological outline will save time, expense, error, and confusion for those you have asked to handle things when you die.

1. Notify immediate family.
2. Secure deed to the family burial plot lot. If not yet issued, locate contract to determine whether additional payment is necessary before interment can be made. A form of interment authorization, available at the funeral director's office, must be signed either by the lot owner or next of kin. The deed, if available, should be presented at the office when the family goes to the cemetery for the interment.
3. Secure will and all insurance policies. It is important to check such papers to see whether the deceased made any specific requests or plans in relation to funeral arrangements.
4. Plan the funeral arrangements.
    (a) Notify funeral director. Show him this book. The funeral director will make all necessary arrangements with the cemetery, obtain a death certificate from the attending physician, prepare all documents necessary for the interment, and arrange for the service, cars, newspaper notice, and so forth.

Mid-Life Crisis

A few years ago, teen-age adolescent growing pains were in vogue. Today the most popular psychoemotional problem is your basic mid-life crisis—and I have it! They say youth is a gift of God but old age is a work of art. Well, then, I'm fast approaching the artistic stage.

Anyway, I'm far enough past forty to be enjoying the extremely popular "mid-life crisis," which is—as the books, magazine articles, my psychiatrist-brother, Bill, and my psychologist-sister, Ranny, all remind me—a crisis of limitations, a time of transition, of self-doubt, of self-acceptance, of search, questions, moods, ambiguities, fears, hopes, and the halting beginnings of a mature peace.

I need to "let go," "let it be," "do it," "relax into reality," accept what is, live now," and seek fulfillment in the unconditional "I-thou" present, no strings attached, batteries not included. This used to be called "growing old gracefully" and, before that, "accepting the will of God."

Those were the days, my friends! When your forties and fifties were the peak of life! Now they are just a mid-life crisis.

Welcome.

(b) Notify the clergyman. Show him the pertinent sections in this book. He will then plan the spiritual part of the rite of passage accordingly. Together with the funeral director and pastor, decide what day and time the funeral will be held, taking into consideration families traveling from out-of-town—and whether the funeral is to be held in the home, a church, or a mortuary chapel.

5. After arrangements have been made, notify other relatives and friends concerning:

    (a) time and place of the funeral service.

    (b) time and place of interment service.

6. Notify attorney, executor, accountant, and insurance companies.

7. Notify benevolent or fraternal organizations and inquire about possible benefits.

8. Notify employer and inquire whether any company benefits are available.

9. Apply for social-security and veterans' benefits. Check for Survivors Pension Program (a kind of life insurance for survivors and also a lump-sum payment for funeral expenses—both available through the Social Security administration).

Empty Heart

Here are ten commandments for when you're left holding an empty heart:

1. Realize and recognize the loss.
2. Take time for nature's slow, sure, stuttering process of healing.
3. Give yourself massive doses of restful relaxation and routine busy-ness.
4. Be vulnerable, share your pain, and be humble enough to accept support.
5. Surround yourself with life: plants, animals, and friends.
6. Use mementos to help your mourning, not to live in the dead past.
7. Avoid rebound relationships, big decisions, and anything addictive.
8. Keep a diary and add up the graces and gifts you have received; forgive.
9. Prepare for change, new interests, new friends, solitude, creativity, growth.
10. Make a personal act of faith and hope: Good Fridays always become Easter Sundays.

Kindly keep the commandments.

Financial Help for Your Survivors

Your Will: Everyone must have a will. If you have not made one, refer to the chapter on "Your Will," consult a lawyer promptly, and then bring it up to date as conditions change. This avoids delay and doubt and provides financial help for those who survive you. It also allows you to distribute your estate as you desire; state law will direct distribution of your assets when there is no will.

Death Benefits: Many death benefits are unclaimed because the survivors are not informed of their availability. Some of the sources are listed below. Check the ones you are entitled to receive. Include details as to source and amount when known.

Social Security: A lump-sum benefit of over $250 is available to the spouse, dependents, or another person paying funeral expenses. Most workers who are covered are entitled to some benefits. Are you covered? yes _____ no _____

Life Insurance: Refer to chapter on "Insurance."

Workman's Compensation Insurance (would apply if occupational factors are involved with your death—which you obviously cannot predict at this point) Are you covered? yes _____ no _____

Employer: _____

131

Financial Help for Your Survivors (cont'd)

State employer compensation: yes ——— no ———

Automobile club insurance: yes ——— no ———

Fraternal organization benefits: yes ——— no ———

Religious group benefits: yes ——— no ———

Health and accident insurance: yes ——— no ———

Medicare: yes ——— no ———

Military veterans benefits: yes ——— no ———

Pensions or annuity payments: yes ——— no ———

Other: _____

_____

P.S. Please include pertinent supporting documents relating to any of the above or indicate here what and where they are.

Chapter 11

YOUR EDUCATION

Growth Groups

Americans today are into self-improvement—compulsively. We are out to change our lives, raise our consciousnesses, lower our blood pressure, accelerate our growing, stop our worrying. We want to become whole, integrated. We want to be happy.

Baretta and bowling, bridge and bingo have been replaced by EST, pottery-making, transcendental meditation, transactional analysis, alpha wave control, Sufi dancing, Scientology, jogging, health foods, biofeedback, yoga, rolfing, mind dynamics, speed reading, assertiveness training, encounter groups, liberation . . . ad finitum.

We're spending countless hours and thousands of dollars to realize our potential to become fully human and alive, to discover true meaning and real happiness—and someone had the nerve to suggest that the whole program was already available in paperback for a mere $1.25. It's called the New Testament. The Gospel good news of Jesus.

Someone else pointed out that the price was ridiculously low; the book and message almost two thousand years old; much too traditional, too old-fashioned.

Now, perhaps, if it could be repackaged in a series of twenty-six religious-education Christian growth sessions, say, for $275, it just might catch on.

About Other Readings

Today there is a growing interest in attitudes toward death —and the publishing industry reflects it. An increasing number of worthwhile books, pamphlets, and articles deal with the subject, both on the adult and child levels. I have picked up almost forty paperback books on dying in the last six months.

Rather than attempting here a complete list of recommended readings and resources—a list that would only be outdated in a matter of months—may I recommend that you consult the card catalogs and listings of new acquisitions at your local public library. Librarians are always glad to help you find what you're looking for if you cannot readily locate it yourself. One of the best bibliographies on death can be found in David Hendin's *Death As a Fact of Life* (New York: Warner, 1973).

A good 550-page overview can be found in editor Edwin S. Shneidman's *Death: Current Perspectives* (Palo Alto, Cal.: Mayfield, 1976). Everyone has heard of Elisabeth Kübler-Ross's pioneering work, *On Death and Dying;* I found her collection of essays, *Death: The Final Stage of Growth* (Englewood Cliffs, N.J.: Prentice-Hall, 1975) equally enlightening. Finally, Sylvia Porter's *New Money Book for the 80's* (New York: Doubleday, 1979) has a comprehensive twenty-five pages on "Wills, Estates, and Trusts"—with several pages of a "checklist for your personal affairs."

Death Around the World

Walking along the beach the other day, I happened upon one of those sand-creations that kids make, only this one wasn't a castle or a fort. It was a tomb. Someone has spent hours building a beautiful little sand cemetery, complete with burial plots and several elaborate sand crosses—the universal Christian symbol of hope for resurrection.

This reminded me of how death customs reflect life culture. For those who see life as a journey, death celebrates passage. For those who see life as a preparation, death celebrates resurrection. For those who see life's values as faith and family, death becomes a celebration of both—faith and family.

In Ireland, sons dig the grave and the family fills the casket with little memorabilia from the person's life (like a clay pipe or a rosary!). And, of course, the Irish are still masters of Christian mourning, especially, at the Wake which is celebrated (really!) at home.

In Spain, on the other hand, death is quite solemn (no drinking); family and friends dig the grave and the whole village proceeds to the cemetery (Spanish people make the sign of the Cross every time they pass a cemetery)—all very earthy and natural; only super-celebrities like Franco get embalmed. Loved ones wear black for at least a year and keep candles burning near photos of those recently deceased.

In Chile, when a child dies, the baby is dressed up like a little angel and placed on a chair near the altar, while a twenty-four-hour dance vigil celebrates resurrection.

America is a very young country. Our traditions, culture, and celebrations are beginning to deepen and take root. We are getting much better at dying.

Some Audiovisual Aids

Ours is an age of communication or, at least, of electronic mass media. Excellent cassette-tape programs are available from the Center for Death Education and Research at the University of Minnesota. The National Funeral Directors Association (135 West Wells St., Milwaukee, WI 53203) also offers a selection of literature and audiovisual materials. The Extension Media Center of the University of California at Berkeley, Cal., 94720, has a helpful videotape library. And Ernest Morgan's valuable little pamphlet, *A Manual of Death Education and Simple Burial* (Burnsville, N.C.: Celo Press, 1975) provides an excellent listing of books, memoirs, films, filmstrips, tapes, and periodicals.

Death in a Foreign Country

About eight thousand Americans die in a foreign country each year. Therefore, every passport should contain special instructions to be followed in case of death—especially if someone is traveling alone.

It costs about $2,500 to fly the body back from Europe, and approximately $3,500 from Asia. Many are therefore buried or cremated in the countries where death takes place.

The United States Consul in that country can and will provide valuable advice and assistance.

A Few Do's

Last Sunday at Mass we passed out little slips of paper to each person, with a special spiritual project. Here are a few for you to choose from:

Mend a quarrel.

Re-establish contact with someone you haven't seen or talked to for over a year.

Do a special act of thoughtfulness at home—and don't tell anyone.

If you ride the bus, give your seat to someone else; if you don't, smile at a stranger.

Dismiss a suspicion—and replace it with trust.

Write a letter to someone who misses you.

Encourage a youth who has lost faith.

Keep a promise.

Forget an old grudge.

Examine your demands on others and vow to reduce them.

Fight for a principle.

Express your gratitude.

Overcome an old fear.

Take two minutes to appreciate the beauty of nature.

Tell someone you love him. Tell him again.

And again.

And again.

Preparing for the Death of
Someone You Love

By now, you have no doubt realized that this little workbook can also be used to prepare for someone else's death,
perhaps someone close to you who is not able to put his or
her own house and life in order. It could be a wonderful,
gentle way of approaching the whole taboo topic of dying.

Besides using the book itself to organize another's preparation for death, if you have brought yourself to do all you
can to get ready for your own death, you automatically
have learned a great deal and will be readier to cope in a
practical everyday way with the death of someone you love.
And, in the process, you will be helping your husband,
your wife, your parent, your family, your children, and
your friends to get ready also both for their deaths and for
yours.

Empty Is Full

His classmates noted that eight-year-old Stephen's mental retardation was becoming even more manifest. Could they retain their love of him as they came to see his difference? In April, the Sunday School teacher asked all eight children in his class to hide within an empty L'eggs pantyhose container one small object that represented the new life in spring. Fearing that Stephen might not have caught on, and not wanting to embarrass him, the teacher had the children place all unlabeled containers on her desk so she could open them. The first had a tiny flower. "What a lovely sign of new life!" The donor could not help but erupt, "I brought that one!"

Next came a rock. That must be Stephen's, since rocks don't symbolize new life. But Billy shouted that his rock had moss on it and moss represented new life. The teacher agreed. A butterfly flew from the third container, and another child bragged that her choice was the best sign of all. The fourth L'eggs container was empty. "It has to be Stephen's," thought the teacher, reaching quickly for a fifth. "Please, don't skip mine," Stephen interjected. "But it's empty." "That's right," said Stephen, "the tomb was empty, and *that's* new life for everyone."

Later that summer Stephen's condition worsened and he died. At his funeral on his casket mourners found eight L'eggs pantyhose containers, now all empty.

Deathbed Promises

Getting ready for death is different from trying to keep control of things from beyond the grave. A tragically common mistake is to exact promises from your grieving children or relatives as you lie dying. This can create guilt feelings later on. It is also manipulative and unfair—even though not intended as such.

Of course, if you get caught in the position of being asked to give such a promise, simply say, "I'll try" instead of, "Yes, I promise." Too many survivors have suffered guilt because of their inability to carry out promises that the dying person would never have asked in his or her right mind.

Why?

Dear Reader or Reporter or Talk Show Host,

You may wonder why I wrote this book. I wrote this book because I am a believer:

I believe that death is real, that it will come to all of us.

I believe that death is unnatural, that it is a horrible, hurting part of our fallen human condition.

I believe that death is frightening, that it evokes deep fascination, awful fear, and sometimes paralyzing pain.

I believe that death must be faced and celebrated, that human beings need ritual passage and commemorative events to handle the overpowering mystery of life and death.

I believe that death is easier when your house is in order, that between a sick, sentimental, ungodly, inhuman experience of death and an honest, healthy, holy celebration of death the difference is preparation.

I believe that death has been and can be overcome—by Christ and in faith, by resurrection and in hope, and through the love of a family.

I pray that this little book will help you and me and others to set our houses and heads and hearts in order.

Documents to Be Attached

		Attached or N/A
1.	Existing wills of both spouses	——
2.	Latest gift-tax returns filed by either spouse	——
3.	Life insurance policies	——
4.	Pension, profit-sharing, or deferred compensation plans	——
5.	Buy/sell or stock redemption agreements	——
6.	Trust instruments	——
7.	Income tax returns for past five years	——
8.	Business agreements and documents regarding interest in corporations, partnerships, and sole proprietorships	——
9.	Pre- or postnuptial agreements	——
10.	Instruments showing basis or assets held	——
11.	Instruments creating spouse's joint tenancies	——
12.	Other documents: _____	——
13.	Papers: _____	——
14.	References: _____	——
15.	Copies: _____	——

It's Not Finished

Once upon a time, the story goes, there was a man who told parables or stories. Wonderful, simple, touching, memorable stories about people—and about what made people sad or happy, angry or forgiving, selfish or loving, nervous or brave, afraid or trusting.

The man's stories were like myths that describe roots and reasons—and like fables that give assurance and encouragement—and like TV commercials that point out human problems and suggest solutions—and like love letters that challenge us to change.

The man's stories were extensions of himself, his life, his mission, his message. Unlike a lot of us, what he said and what he did were in sync, together.

So much so, that the best story the man ever told was his own: his living and dying and living forever. Near the end he said, "It is finished," when it had only just begun. Just like us. He was dying and his thirty-three years were ending. He was scared to die.

He had not stopped believing in his Father and hoping in life. We are all planting seeds that won't grow until we are gone. Maybe things blossom better when we're not watching: kettles, children, communities, creeds.

He cried, "It is finished," because that's the way he felt. And that's the way we feel. Only faith enables us to transcend appearances and feelings.

The alternative, eventually, is despair.

I would rather believe in beginnings and finishings, in dyings and risings, and in love stories without end.

After the Dust Settles

A final suggestion would be to encourage everyone to talk as freely and honestly about death as he or she can—especially to bereaved families and to children. Don't be nervous about approaching either the topic of death or those who have recently lost someone. Your concern, your fearlessness will inevitably comfort—except in those cases where someone refuses to let go of the dead person and continues to wallow in prolonged grief or abnormal self-pity.

The age of hush-hush, pretend-it-isn't-there reticence about the reality of death is over. As we face and accept death, life becomes more meaningful. And it's not too big or difficult a step from faith in life to hope in resurrection.

Pope John XXIII summed it up just before he died in 1963: "Any day is a good day to be born. Any day is a good day to die. I'm ready. My bags are packed."

And now your bags are packed—you have set your house in order.

NOTES

NOTES

NOTES

NOTES

NOTES

NOTES

NOTES

NOTES

NOTES

NOTES